Extended Family

Combining Ages
in Church Experience

Lela Hendrix

BROADMAN PRESS
Nashville, Tennessee

© Copyright 1979 • Broadman Press.
All rights reserved.
4234-26
ISBN: 0-8054-3426-7

To John
who for twenty years has run out before me,
beckoned me to him,
taken my hand,
and walked beside me.

Dewey Decimal Classification: 268
Subject heading: RELIGIOUS EDUCATION
Library of Congress Catalog Card Number: 78-59278
Printed in the United States of America

Contents

Learning Is Informal
Learning Is from Friends and Models
Learning Is Reflecting on Experiences
Learning Is Planned

Preface

I want to share something good with you. If I sound proud of the extended family model of combining all ages in church experience, it is because I have been both an observer and participant, and I know the concept is worth sharing.

Many people have participated in the building of these basic beliefs and assumptions. When the term "Second Family" is found in the book, it refers to specific extended family groups that have been beginning and ending since the spring of 1974. The first Second Family began in the Immanuel Baptist Church, Nashville, Tennessee. Two other Nashville churches have formed extended family groups within their congregations—the Bellevue Baptist Church and Glendale Baptist Church. Many of the assumptions, evaluations, and program suggestions have come from the creative persons who shared the leadership of these groups. It would be impossible to name each one who contributed ideas to the extended family model, but these nameless persons are of all ages—from four years to seventy-plus years.

In 1976, the Church Training Department of the Sunday School Board of the Southern Baptist Convention became interested in the extended family concept and included this intergenerational model as one short-term study in the Equipping Center pilot project. Two hundred churches in five states were offered the opportunity of trying two different intergenerational learning modules. The evaluations from the testing program have helped to discriminate between those features of the extended family design that were most useful in the local church and those which were difficult to implement. In the summer of 1976, Second Family groups were formed at each of the two Baptist Conference Centers—Ridgecrest, North Carolina, and Glorieta, New Mexico. These six-day training sessions indicated that the same ideas that were working in the local church could also be utilized in the seminar or retreat setting.

The churches, leaders, and participants who have been involved in learning together what an extended family could be in the church are to be praised and complimented for their endeavors.

My personal appreciation is given . . .

. . . to John, my husband, who has been the creator and innovator of much of the extended family model. His modesty will prevent him from owning up to the leadership role; but in his own catalytic way, he has started the creativity rolling within many of us who wanted and needed an extended family group. He was ready to give suggestions and support whenever I needed it.

. . . to Melissa and Jud, our children, I owe many hugs and kisses for their patience in "leaving mother alone so she can work on the book." Their insights and comments about experiences in Second Family events have been valuable in seeing a "child's viewpoint."

. . . to Roy and Lena Dilcom, my parents, and my brother, Leonard, I express gratitude for my positive feelings about what a family can be. I remember many good things about being in my family of origin. I wish that every child could really know a little of the love and security I was given.

. . . to three families, who continue to be in our extended family network through the years and across the miles, I give my thanks and love that they are there when I need them—the Lee family, the Rushing family, and the Scarborough family.

1
All God's Children:
Search for an Extended Family

> *And so we should not be like cringing, fearful slaves, but we should behave like God's very own children, adopted into the bosom of his family, and calling to him, "Father, Father." For his Holy Spirit speaks to us deep in our hearts, and tells us that we really are God's children. And since we are his children, we will share his treasures—for all God gives to his Son Jesus is now ours too.*
>
> *Romans 8:15-17*

As I sat down for my second cup of morning coffee, I picked up the daily paper and began to glance through the pages. I skimmed quickly over the headlines and lead sentences. My eyes came to a sudden halt at an unusual article title: "(Ad) option Offered for Grandparents." The story told of a young couple in Michigan who were advertising in the classified section of their local newspaper for a set of grandparents. This father and mother had two young children who were missing the privilege of seeing their own sets of grandparents. In an attempt to get the young children together with the older generation, the parents were hoping to find some older grandparent-type adults who would like to share their life. The story said that several responses had been received to the ad—*Wanted: Grandparents.*

Upon reading the story, I stopped to think about my own family situation . . .

. . . I thought about our separation from other members of our original families—our parents, our sisters and brothers. It had been years since John or I had spent more than a few days with any of the persons that had been such an intricate part of our life in the past. Our lives did not include them anymore, or so it seemed.

. . . I thought about our children and how they were growing up in what is called a "nuclear" family. They were surounded with neighborhood friends and adults, school-teachers, and church acquaintances of all ages. They were not by any means lacking for outside influences and, yet, I knew they had few opportunities to be close to people who were like extended family. They certainly never talked about spending Friday night with grandma and grandpa or spending a week next summer with Uncle Leonard's or Aunt Carrah's family. The relationships of our nuclear family were bound together within the circle of the four of us. The postal service, telephone calls, and yearly visits were the children's methods of developing extended family ties and bonds.

. . . I thought about the times that as a mother of two young children I would have welcomed the support of family members. At most times I was self-sufficient because I learned that I needed to be that way. I knew that John and I both were taking seriously our responsibility of providing a home for our family and I was not asking for financial support, or emotional support, or moment-by-moment directions for living my life. I was just thinking it would just be nice to have a variety of people who were like family who could say, "Hey, I remember when . . ." or "I hope it will be like . . ."

. . . I thought about the concept of the "model" family that I had built through the years of reading books and viewing television. Our family could pass for the ideal family. We were like the family in the first-grade textbooks of the

1940s—Dick, Jane, Mother, Father, Spot—the dog, and Puff—the cat. One exception! We only had the dog! The model family on the television set played ball together, took walks in the park, and ate fortified cereal for breakfast. The father worked downtown to support the family and the mother cooked great meals, laundered the clothes with the best detergent, and waxed the floors of their suburban home. Yes, we fit the role of the model family.

. . . I thought again about the couple in Michigan who had advertised for others to share their life. I could identify with their dilemma and I knew what they were doing. They were searching. *Searching for an extended family!*

Searching for Something

"Excuse me, Sir, I think I've lost something."

"Yes, maybe I can help. What is it that you have lost?"

"Well, you see, Sir, it is rather difficult to tell you what I've lost because I'm not sure that I had it. I think I have had it, but I don't know if I can describe it to you. Do you know what I mean?"

"No, I think you will have to be more definite about what you had."

To search for something that is indescribable presents a barrier to finding the object of the search. Through the years, it has been difficult to explain the feelings of community and family that we experienced. We did not know how to describe our loss. We only knew the lack of close relationships was causing unrest.

With the assistance of friends from our church and our work, we began to piece together the puzzle of times, places, and persons who had provided us with the extended family relationships that were beneficial to our growth as persons. We discovered that this extended family had taken over even before we began leaving our families of origin and that this family was not always composed of persons related by blood or marriage.

The persons who were our extended family were found within the context of our church, work, and school world. These persons became older brothers, younger brothers, sisters, father-like figures, sister-mother combinations, grandmothers and grandfathers . . . . We spent time around the table—eating meals, drinking coffee, sharing pot-luck when none of us alone had enough food to prepare a balanced meal . . . . We confessed together—deeds from our past that had been shared with no other persons. Forgiveness and acceptance were experienced from our brothers and sisters in Christ. . . . Frustrations of the day were relieved by the verbal telling of the pressures and demands . . . . Our limitations were confronted while loving hands held ours . . . . In joys and sorrows, arms extended that folded us inside.

Explaining the past is difficult. Only from your experience and your heart will you, the reader, be able to understand the object of the search. The search is an experiential search and is similar, yet different, for each person. Our common experience from the past is that to some degree or another we have shared life with other people. Dietrich Bonhoeffer in *Life Together,* says:

There is probably no Christian to whom God has not given the uplifting *experience* of genuine Christian community at least once in his life. But in this world such experiences can be no more than a gracious extra beyond the daily bread of Christian community life. [1]

There is no way of accurately predicting what kind of past experience stimulates persons to seek familial relationships beyond their family of origin or immediate family. Many persons who have been through negative experiences never want to be related to anything that reminds them of the family bond, or so they say. Other people reach out for the positive relationships they never had. Some people who speak of close familial ties are not eager to become a part of new family-like relationships. Perhaps everything was so good the first time they are not willing to risk a mediocre or not-so-good experience. On the other hand, there are individuals who seek to share from their overflow. They know a good thing when they have it and want to "do it again."

Why are you interested in the extended family concept? Have you defined your reasons for searching? Are you curious? Are you looking for something to fill a vaccum? Are you willing to share life because of an overflow of love?

The Search Becomes More Intense

In the fall season of 1973, the Hendrix family seriously began to search for an extended family. We began to talk about our desire to find persons within our local church congregation who would be interested in sharing some time each week for the purpose of doing family activities. We talked about building a group that would look like an extended family.

During that fall season, we also began looking for a man who would be a "substitute" father for five-year-old Jud. Jud would be leaving the extended nursery session to enter the Sunday morning worship; and since John and I were members of the adult choir, we needed someone to sit with him. Melissa, who was seven years old at that time, was already sitting with the pastor's wife. Mary Catherine McGlothlen, lovingly called "Mama Mac," had a small group of little girls who sat with her each Sunday. She guided and watched over them as their parents sang in the choir. Because Jud was entering this new phase of his church life, we were concerned that he find someone to share these important events of worship with him.

With these needs in our lives, we began to search for people who would understand with their minds and hearts. Our needs were "heard" by Mabel and Albert McClellan. Albert volunteered to shepherd Jud. In the years that followed, Jud not only found someone who would sit with him in church, but he found a grandfather-figure, who is known to all of us as "Abba."

In the McClellans, John and I found two adults who were willing to share their experience and insights. They would join our efforts. Looking back to those "beginning days," Abba and Mabel share the following reasons for being drawn to the extended family concept:

"1. There has been a growing conviction in our minds that the separation of the ages in the church is sometimes artificial and unreal. It departmentalizes the age grouping, so they have little opportunity of meeting other people or learning about other people. This is especially damaging to children. We felt that a more natural situation would be in some cases to have all the ages together for maximum maintenance of the human spirit.

"2. Young people were losing interest in some phases of our church life. We felt this was because they did not know older people, so when the extended family was proposed, we saw it as an opportunity for ministry to young people and to children.

"3. Growing older one senses a certain loss of resilience and he suspicions that the reason may be that there has been a loss of contact with youth. Because of this when the idea of the extended family was proposed, we decided to try to regain our resilience by engaging in this fellowship. We can truthfully say that it was rewarding at this point far beyond our hopes. We found new resilience in contact with younger people.

"4. Our church has come to a time when we need new ideas and new forms of meeting. Some people are content with the old, others are not. We found in this great opportunity to enlist new people in Church Training and to extend the ministry of learning and study to people that have not been previously enrolled. Here again we succeeded very well. Since our first experience about four years ago we have been in several of these families and always we have found them to be inspiring and life giving."

Once a decision was made to take an active role in designing an extended family experience within the church structure, excitement began to build. Some of the preliminary steps in the months prior to our first session included securing permission and acceptance from the church staff and Sunday night program personnel; pulling together a list of families who might be interested; and making written, telephone, and personal contacts concerning the idea. The most workable time slot in which to schedule this family-life education group was within the Sunday night Church Training period from 7:00 to 8:00. The months of February, March, April, and May were selected and the Fellowship Hall of Immanuel Baptist Church, Nashville, Tennessee, was the primary meeting place.

The name "Second Family" was given to the group in lieu of calling it an intergenerational group (too big a word) or extended family (too general).

Several weeks before the first session, announcements were placed in the Sunday church bulletin giving information about the new group that was forming and inviting anyone who was interested to join. Although intentional planning had been done in enlisting families that would provide a balanced distribution of ages, the Second Family was not to be a closed group by any means. At the first session we had individuals and families attend who had come only through the invitation in the bulletin. They came because something about a family group sparked a need or desire in them.

The first session was hectic. The people who were invited came—single adults, families with children, couples without any children, teenagers without any parents. There was a four-year-old boy and a retired seminary professor of seventy plus years—with all ages in between represented. The room filled and the tables of ten became tables with twelve. The room became too warm, too noisy, too chaotic. There was singing, laughing, shouting, and praying. As the forty or more persons left the room after the first hour, the McClellans and John and I sat down and pondered the situation.

Would it work? There were several preschoolers that could not read yet. There were teenagers who looked a little ill-at-ease with the whole thing. There were professional men and women—many with earned doctorates. There were adults with years of experiences. Would it work? Is it possible to keep the interest of little boys and older women together on the same topic? Will a ten-year-old girl be able to work at an activity with a fifty-eight year old man who has been just someone she sees in the hallway on Wednesdays and Sundays? Can the seven-year-old call the adult by his first name? Will the adult *let* the child call him by the first name only?

Would it work? The questions came! The intervening week was one of intrigue. Would anyone return for the second session? Would they bring their calendars and work out a three-month program which would include all generations? Would they commit themselves to attending—regardless of what happened? Would they commit themselves to planning and leading at least one session?

Instead of using only one section of Fellowship Hall for the second meeting, the entire room was opened wide to provide ample space. The people came back. They stopped at the refreshment table and clustered in small groups—the adults in their groups, the teenagers in their groups, the younger children running and chasing throughout the room. At the signal to find a table, additional instructions were provided so that the adults, youth, and children became more intermingled. The plan was that no one age group become too heavily concentrated at any one activity table. They would learn through the months that Second Family meant all ages *together* not all ages *segregated*.

The weeks passed from winter into spring. The intergenerational group began to be recognized around the church as the Second Family. There was a feeling that persons involved were becoming a distinct group and by the end of May, there came a sense of direction for what an intergenerational group could or could not be.

"Second Family did this . . ." and "Second Family did that . . . ." The excitement of being in this family group spread. Other people wanted to try duplicating what had been done. At that time, all we had to share were a simple outline of each session, a few suggestions for methodology, several pages of evaluation statements from the participants, and verbal encouragement that the model would be successful. As reports came back from other groups, it was obvious that more how-to information and resources were needed. Family-life education in the churches was becoming more popular but much of the published material was geared to specific age groups. In reviewing the program ideas and resources that were available, it was apparent that some ideas were useable in the church but many suggestions were designed to be used in the home setting. There remained a void in the area of what to do with all ages mixed together at the church. Our search turned in the direction of how to provide curriculum and resource materials for churches.

The Search Shared with Others

Although no one group can be a cure-all for the problem caused by the lack of an extended family system, the inter-generational group which focuses on familial relationships can be a positive experience for individuals. Because of this belief that something good can happen from such a group, it is with much eagerness that the findings from our personal search be shared. The search revealed that . . .

. . . The extended family experience is capable of becoming a dynamic, caring fellowship.

How does one explain the creativity that comes out of the family members when the assignment is given to create a simple art form? How does one explain the urge that causes the small hand of the child to reach up to clasp the wrinkled hand of the older woman. How does one explain the current that passes from the older man to the younger boy as the man's hand gently pats the shoulder of the lad.

Persons who have shared in extended family events speak of a dynamic that is present—a force and power that they have experienced. Many members recognize that the skillful use of small-group techniques and experiential teaching methods help in forming the participants into an intimate, caring fellowship. Christian group members are aware of a special element—the dynamic power and presence of the Holy Spirit.

Little children, yet a little while I am with you. You will seek me; and as I said to the Jews so now I say to you, 'Where I am going you cannot come.' A new commandment I give to you, that you love one another; even as I have loved you, that you also love one another. By this all men will know that you are my disciples, if you have love for one another (John 13:33-35, RSV).

The words of Jesus call us to search for ways to live out his commandment. The extended family group is one of these ways.

> . . . *the extended family, as an intergenerational group, is a viable option for meeting the objectives of the religious education ministry of the local church.*

The original Second Family group was designed to meet certain objectives which were:

1. To discover an optional way of enlisting the total family in the training program of the church.
2. To enlist persons who are not part of on-going or short-term groups.
3. To provide an intergenerational group of persons that fosters personal, family, and church enrichment and growth.
4. To provide extended families for persons outside normally-functioning family settings.
5. To provide opportunities for persons to choose a broader relational pattern with other church members.
6. To provide models for more meaningful Christian education in the home.

These objectives present general, but realistic, goals for an intergenerational group that functions alongside the age-graded and sex-graded groups already in existence within the educational program. An extended family is suggested as an alternative, optional method of organizing a group. The six objectives above are not comprehensive. They could be expanded as a church focuses on its own particular purposes for such a group. On the other extreme, the objectives might be too general or too many in number. A church might have only one or two specific reasons for providing intergenerational or extended family groups for the members.

> *. . . an extended family group is an environmental setting wherein potential familial relationships are discovered and nurtured.*

The physical and social environment are involved in the choices of one's friends, neighbors, and fellow church members. In the search for persons who could share life, where would you look for these persons? Would you advertise at random in the local newspaper as the couple in Michigan did? Would you look for persons in the local shopping mall and approach them about sharing life?

In the search for extended family, many people state they would like to find persons to share life from the places that are already a part of their environment. The local church congregation is one such place for discovering relationships. The extended family setting is created to help relationships be found and nurtured. There is no guarantee that everyone will find a lifelong friend and brother. No group can promise that. The extended family concept is designed to provide the possibility.

> *. . . The extended family experience is a challenging teaching and learning model for the smaller church or intergenerational organization.*

"Small is beautiful" is a phrase which developed to counter balance the pressure of "bigger and better." Sometimes small is beautiful and sometimes being small can be a problem. For a church whose attendance is sixty and below and contains a mixture of all ages, there can be a dilemma of how to plan the programs using ideas and materials that are designed for churches with larger numbers of people.

Within the larger church, there can develop a need for intergenerational programming when one or two organizations have a "slump" in attendance or when the enrollment falls below the level where age-graded divisions are work-able.

Sometimes there comes a negative feeling when the numbers are lower than what is expected. Then there comes the time when reality must be faced. One church which has a functioning age-graded program every Sunday night during the fall, winter, and spring months faces a usual summer slump. The positive approach has been to face the problem and work on it. The extended family programming was a way of combining all the children, some of the teenagers, and one of the adult groups into a family-like group. The extended family concept provided the structure around which the programming was accomplished. The family group spent their time together "doing what families do." When the vacation and travel period ended, the intergenerational group dissolved to begin the age-graded program for the next nine months.

Intergenerational grouping has presented new challenges to some church leaders because the concept is quite different from the regular age-graded programming. The lack of ongoing curriculum and plentiful resource materials means that more creativity must be used in keeping these groups alive. The church family, like the family in the home, seems to have forgotten how to do things together when placed in the same setting. Relearning must take place. When staff and lay leaders become convinced of the extended family concept, they can and do build very effective groups. From the trial and error experiences of the churches and organizations who are trying extended family groups and other intergenerational events, there is developing a body of materials and assumptions for this approach to learning and teaching.

. . the extended family experience is an enrichment group for families and is not a therapy group.

Although many families could benefit greatly from a sound, thorough therapy program, the extended family group in the church is not intended for that purpose. The target group is for persons who are *not* "head-over-heels" in problems and misery. Are there any families left who qualify? Sure, the target group contains myriads of families who are asking questions about family life concerns and who are desiring involvement in intergenerational groups.

Family life and segregation of the generations are popular and current topics of concern. Look at the book shelves and magazine racks—anything written about the family, age segregation, and the passages from one age to another are best sellers. The new therapeutic approaches in the journals and textbooks are not just regular family therapy, but network intervention for families, multi-family group therapy, and conjoint family therapy. The consciousness-raising is working. Families are seeking help. A few large churches provide therapy programs and private counseling, but most church members who want therapy must go to community agencies or private counselors.

Therapy, prevention, and enrichment—the movement from crisis to wholeness is a growing concern for churches. Preventive measures and support groups for families will become more available in the future as churches find new opportunities for enriching the lives of church families. The extended family experience is designed to aid in the ministry of enrichment.

> . . . *an extended family experience can be successfully geared to the child's level of understanding and still involve youth and adults.*

Secrets. Everyone loves secrets. If there was one secret that would keep the extended family concept from being successful, it would be: *the child is the key.* In combining ages for a learning experience in the church, the child's level must be the focal point. There are some things children cannot do. They cannot understand all that the youth and adults can understand. They cannot operate on the level above where they are. They can operate only at their level—as a child. And that is the secret of building an extended family experience. Base the learning on the level of the younger members. Keep the concepts simple—make the abstract into concrete. Keep the learning activity-oriented. Talk less, do more!

The idea sounds good, doesn't it? But does it work? How can the trained, well-educated, sophisticated adult keep an interest in a group that only does things for children? The truth is that not all well-educated, sophisticated adults will be able to sustain membership in an intergenerational group. There are some adults who cannot work in the area of their "child." The writings of the transactional analysis literature explaining the "adult," "parent," and "child" that operate within each individual are beneficial in understanding an intergenerational model of learning and relating. (See Additional Resources for further study in transactional analyis.)

When the adult and youth can "get hold of the child that is within," then any activity or concept can be met on the common ground of the youngest child in the group.

There are some areas where the child and adult are on a mutual level—feelings, for example. All ages feel hurt, sadness, joy, gladness. In fact, the child might even surpass the adult in the ability to openly and honestly express feelings.

The design for mixing all ages together pivots on the ability to share experiences that everyone, even the child, can identify with and understand. Gearing to the child's level presupposes that some topics will not be studied in the intergenerational group. Einstein's general theory of relativity is out.

So are some of the highly abstract philosophies which many
adults spend time in discussing. Fortunately, the basics of
the Christian's life are teachable to the young and old. We
can find many concrete methods for teaching love, forgiveness, equality, justice, and the other essentials of the faith.
Jesus taught us how. So the secret is out! Gear to the child's
level!

> . . . *the extended family group can function without the
> threat of it becoming a "little church" within the
> church.*

"Please, don't let the extended family group leave the
church and start meeting in homes. Don't become another
group that does not support the local congregation by meeting elsewhere."

Some families are meeting in homes for similar extended
family experiences; however, the model in this book is designed to function within the physical facility and organiza-
tional structure of the local church.

The extended family may give the appearance of a "little
church" because it offers a variety of experiences in education, worship, and fellowship—experiences that are akin to
the total program of the church, except on a limited scale.
Although the building of a sense of community and fellowship among the family members is strong, the possibility
of the group becoming a threat to the well-being of the
church is small. Built into the model is the assumption that
this is an open group, not a closed group. No one is "shut
out." The group also has a beginning and ending, allowing
some persons to leave and others to enter. Because the needs
of families and individuals change, the need for the extended
family group is not the same as the need for the church.
The extended family group is to be church-like but is not
intended to become the church.

2
Members of Many Families:
Tasks of the Extended Family

Reflections on a Family
—baby
—5
—10
—teens
—20
—married
—children
—children grow
—children have children
—grandma
—great grandma
—1 more year
—dead

Melissa Hendrix, age 7

The Family System

Family—a simple word that symbolizes a complex system. The family—an ancient, well-established institution that is a part of everyone's experience. Although no one claims to have knowledge of the exact point in time for the origin of the family system, almost every identifiable society developed some form of family life. There are even studies to suggest that the higher animals lived in families before the human race existed.

Families and society are closely related and interdependent. The society is a larger version of the family. The forming and training that take place in the families will be reflected in the kind of society that is created—the government, the schools, the agencies, the church, and certainly the extended family group in the church.

The family is a smaller version of the society. The individual members of the family will be influenced by the surroundings in which they are located. Like concentric circles in a whirlpool, families are influenced by the society closest to them—neighborhood, city, state, nation—and via media, by societies that surround the world. The phrase "It's a small world" is interesting in the light of family patterns. The future alone can answer the question: Will families and family systems begin to merge and look more alike or will they begin to close their rank and file and seek to maintain separate, distinct identities?

One way to picture the family is symbolized by the circle. We hear the phrase "family circle." The circle implies unity, wholeness, continuity, overlap, and neverendedness. These qualities are lofty and abstract. They are qualities which suggest an ideal of what the family should be.

Another way to visualize the family is by the "family tree"—the roots and branches stretch out to include many members. The tree symbol is earthy. The tree is used to graph a particular family or a larger group, like a clan.

The use of a pictorial symbol may be helpful in gaining a perspective for this study. The focus of this book is on forming an extended family which is not necessarily blood related. To design a model of an extended family group, it is necessary to consider the family groupings which are important to the participants. To depict how the extended family experience relates to other family groups, the symbols of the circle and tree are combined into one symbol. The family system is symbolized by the tree. The interacting family groups are symbolized in the overlapping circles.

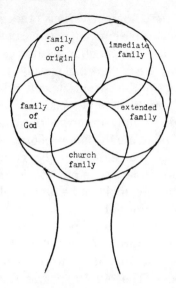

An extended family has a role in both the spiritual and natural family systems. In the natural family system, the extended family is composed of nuclear (immediate) families who are bound together by marriage or blood to a family of origin. The extended family group is the largest group because it is a sum of the many parts.

In the spiritual family system of a Christian, the extended family is a small family group within the church family. The church family is a smaller version of the family of God. Persons hold membership in a number of extended family groups—by blood and marriage and/or by conviction and relationship.

The Family of Origin

The term family of origin is commonly used to mean the family group in which one lived as a child. As a person leaves the family of the childhood and begins to establish a household, there comes a need to have a title for the family group of the past. The family of origin may be the biological parents and their offspring or one of various other groupings such as: adoptive or foster parents, surrogate (substitute) parents, and/or institutions that function as homes for parentless children. Siblings may be biologically related, related through marriages of the parents, legally related, or merely related through emotional and social ties.

In the extended family group in the church, the adult members are asked to use the family of origin as a foundation for their present involvement in the group. "Memories, memories, dreams of days gone by." Remembering the family of the past is one tool for helping adults to relate to the children of the present.

One middle-aged man was speaking of his aging father and of the father's desire to keep telling stories of his past. The son said he and his family were so tired of hearing the same episodes. The old father was disappointed that no one wanted to listen anymore. And, then, there is the small child who begs the parents to "tell me a story about when you were young." The parents who are sometimes too busy to oblige the child may wish for someone to step in and tell the children of by-gone days. In the extended family group, the young and old are encouraged to "ask" and "tell" about the common paths they have trod. Being a child is a common experience.

Adult members of the extended family group can remember and speak of their family of origin. But what about the youth and children? Do they have a family of the past? Yes, but for most of them, the family of origin will also be the immediate family.

The Immediate Family

"But anyone who won't care for his own relatives when they need help, especially those living in his own family, has no right to say he is a Christian. Such a person is worse than the heathen" (1 Tim. 5:8).

Who are the people in your family? If you had a family portrait taken today, who would be included? What do you reply when someone asks, "How many are in your family?" To whom are you responsible? For whom are you responsible?

The immediate family, in the past, usually referred to the parents and their offspring who lived together in a household. The romantic model of the immediate family—mother, father, and the children—is quickly becoming obsolete and, rightly so, because there are other variations of the immediate family. For example, not all immediate families contain children.

The immediate family is sometimes called the nuclear family, which, in the past, has been defined as the parents and their children living separate from other relatives. Obviously, this traditional definition must be revised.

As the extended family experience is developed and promoted within the church, the immediate families for whom it is designed will be defined as person(s) who are presently living together in a household. The following list contains examples of how some immediate family groupings will be arranged within the households:

- two parents with their children (biological and/or adopted)
- single parent with children (biological and/or adopted)
- parents with children no longer in residence
- single, never-married adult
- single, no-longer married adult
- married adults, no children
- grandparent(s) as major caretakers of their grandchildren
- foster home; adults and children who may not be biologically related or legally joined together
- institutional homes: adults, children, and youth related by particular needs—mental, physical, social, etc.

In the Christian households of the apostolic, early church period, the "extra" people who lived with the immediate family were considered a part of the household and were not appendages. The emotional involvements in the early Christian households may not have included equal or proportionate love and attachment, but the concern for the welfare of the individuals was manifested in "family-like" ways.

In the present and future, churches need to recognize combinations of persons, other than blood-related or the parent-child combinations as immediate family. The ministry and outreach of the extended family group in the church is intended to draw in the "household"—or any part of a household.

The nuclear family will be defined in the broader sense as one or more persons who are presently living alone or with others in a household which is separate from other relatives.

The Extended Family

The extended family is usually defined as the network of nuclear families and related individuals who are from two or more generations. The ages in the extended family range from very old to very young and the ties are from blood kin and marriage. As with the immediate families, there is much variation in the networks of extended families.

As we look at the needs of people today there is a recognition that some persons are lacking in natural extended family networks. Even if one wanted to go back to the good old days of family life with all the relatives and loved ones near by, there is no way we can be assured the attempt would be successful. To make the immediate family and extended family needs fit into the old molds is probably not possible. Neither can we assume that a simulated extended family

group will work for everyone or be like the "real thing."
What we can assume is that some families are lacking an
adequate extended family during certain phases of their life
and that family-like groups serve to meet some of the needs
of these individuals.

The persons who join extended family experiences in the
church bring to these intergenerational groups their memories, hopes, dreams, and wishes of what a natural extended
family is. Given support, guidance, and encouragement, the
nuclear families can form themselves into an extended family network that seeks to meet some of the personal needs
at a specific period in life. The extended family composed
of members of God's family seeks to replace or fill the void
caused by the lack of a natural family network. The spiritual
extended family includes the added dimension of being eternal because many of its membership have claimed the promise of life everlasting.

"My Extended Family"

Who are the people in your extended family? Are they relatives?
Are they a mixture of related and non-related individuals? Diagram
your extended family.

On a sheet of paper, place a bubble in the middle. Write your
name on this circle for it represents you. Think of the persons who
are in your extended family. Draw bubbles for each of these people.
If the relationship is strong and intense, draw the bubbles for these
persons closest to yours. Draw bubbles farther away from yours for
individuals who are not so close or so significant. Write the names
of the extended family members on all the bubbles you have drawn.

Now that you have identified the people, determine which ones
are related by blood or marriage. From your bubble to their bubbles,
draw solid lines. Next determine which people are not relatives or
kin. Draw a dotted line from your bubble to their bubbles.

With one other person, or in a small group, discuss your diagram.
Think about these people and their relationship to you. Who are the
people closest to you? Why are they important? Who are the people
fartherest from you? Were you closer to these persons five or ten

years ago? Why? Does your extended family meet your needs? If not, what will you do about your situation?

The Family of God

"For you have a new life. It was not passed on to you from your parents, for the life they gave you will fade away. This new one will last forever, for it comes from Christ, God's ever-living Message to men" (1 Pet. 1:23).

Just as we are born into an earthly family, so we are born into the family of God. "Born again!" exclaimed Nicodemus. "What do you mean? How can an old man go back into his mother's womb and be born again?" (John 3:4).

Jesus's words to Nicodemus caused him to exclaim and confess confusion over the process of being born again. But Jesus assured him that the second birth would be different. In the first epistle of Peter, we are reminded that our life and the lives of our earthly family members will fade away as the grass of the field, but the new life with its new relationships in God's family will last forever.

When I was a child and had not developed the ability to think in lofty, abstract terms, the story of Jesus turning away from his earthly mother and brothers made me sad. (Read Matt. 12:46-50.) It was hard to understand. Why would Jesus not go out to speak with those who were so much a part of his life? How could any person leave the family into which one was born? "I could never do what Jesus did," I said from my childhood point of reference. As my understanding developed and as my own relationships extended outward to those beyond my mother, father, and brother of childhood days, the words and actions of Jesus began to take on more meaning. For Jesus knew that earthly relationships would fade and die like the grass of the field. He knew something else. He knew of the possibility of having lasting relationships here on earth with persons who were a part of God's family. He was aware that some relationships could go on forever. Have you and I realized that yet?

In a sermon, I heard a statement to the effect that "God has no grandchildren." Coming into God's family is on a personal basis and we come as sons and daughters. Jesus becomes our "elder brother." (Read again Rom. 8:15-17.) The family of God becomes ours through our choice and not by inheritance from our earthly parents. We become a part of a spiritual family. We begin to experience on earth some of the relationships that are everlasting. To have fellowship on earth with *all* the numberless members of God's family is impossible. How, then, can we be the family? How is it possible to experience a part of God's family?

Most of us, as Christians, can recall other Christians who are now scattered around the world. Our minds link us to people who are like brothers and sisters and fathers and mothers—family who have been a part of our lives but who are now somewhere else. These people that we know personally help us to grasp the concept that God's family is everywhere. These people that we know represent the countless others who are in our spiritual family. Paul mentions this family in Ephesians 3:14-15. Out of his suffering he spoke of "the Father of all the great family of God—some of them already in heaven and some down here on earth." Our memories of Christians who are alive and of Christians who have died help us to conceptualize the largeness of God's family.

The Church Family

"Praise God for the privilege of being in Christ's family and being called by his wonderful name!" (1 Pet. 4:16).

In the midst of terror, persecution, and death, the first people called "Christian" banded together into households of faith for support, encouragement, fellowship, and worship. Since there were no "houses of worship," the early Christians worshiped in private homes. The New Testament mentions some of these households. One interesting story is recorded in Acts 20. Paul was visiting a household in the city of Troas.

On Sunday, we gathered for a communion service, with Paul preaching. And since he was leaving the next day, he talked until midnight! The upstairs room where we met was lighted with many flickering lamps; and as Paul spoke on and on, a young man named Eutychus, sitting on the window sill, went fast asleep and fell three stories to his death below. Paul went down and took him into his arms. "Don't worry," he said, "he's all right!" And he was! What a wave of awesome joy swept through the crowd! They all went back upstairs and ate the Lord's Supper together; then Paul preached another long sermon—so it was dawn when he finally left them! (Acts 20:7-12).

Modest Christian households lit their lamps and opened their doors to the brothers and sisters of the faith. Apparently, one of the brothers must have been young and tired and even the preaching of Paul was not enough to keep him awake. Falling asleep in church is still happening today, with the difference being that the apostle Paul is not physically present to awaken the dead and sleeping.

The early households of faith were more than buildings and upper chambers. The households, the people themselves, were the temples of God. "The living building-stones" mentioned in 1 Peter 2:4-5, were not bound together by cement and mortar, but were bound together by love and concern. They were trying to live out a new way of life. This new way of being "family" was based on faith in Jesus and love for each other.

As the Christian church developed through the years, the households of faith became identified with specific buildings and structures. However, the "family" concept remained. The nuclear families that composed the congregations became known as a spiritual family. The church of today is spoken of as family—the church family.

The church, as family, has a responsibility to the system around which it is organized. The church then cannot abandon the individuals who are looking to it for help with their needs. When all other organizations that cater to families begin to drop away, the church must and will stand with the family.

The church cannot abandon the family—the parents or the children. In 1977, the Carnegie Corporation, concluded a five-year study on children, with their report entitled *All Our Children: The American Family Under Pressure.* The study recommended that the plight of the American parent must be improved before the nation's children could be helped. The study suggested measures for helping parents through radical overhaul of public policies. Reports from the private sector and any efforts by the government to improve the quality of life for families is always encouraging.

While these studies and suggestions for aid were being reported, the news media kept Americans abreast of the trends that continue to plague family life. A look at events in 1978 reveals some of the trends.

- In Denver, a letter to the editor of *The Denver Post* expressed concern that many apartment complexes in the city were saying "No Children Allowed." Families needing housing are being excluded because children, like pets, are too much trouble for the landlords.

- In many cities across the nation, the public schools are facing a financial crisis because taxpayers are asking that money from their tax dollars not be spent on education for the young. In the fall of 1978 in Nashville, Tennessee, an effort was made by some citizens to have one and one-half cent sales tax taken off the taxation level. Any decrease in tax dollars meant the school systems must come up with millions of dollars from some other source. How soon the adults who do not have children in school forget what education entails and what it means for the society as a whole.

- Alongside the news stories of schools and service agencies who are in financial trouble are horror tales of children who are found in homes where physical abuse is the everyday occurrence. On the flip side of child abuse are stories telling of youth murdering their teachers, their local service station attentant, or store owners, and, yes, even murdering their parents.

The church is not isolated from the culture and it cannot ignore the negative influences on the nuclear families who compose the church family. The church as an organization must continue to minister to families and support family life in order to offset the instability caused from other segments of the environment.

The church cannot ignore the changing patterns of the extended family network. Not every child in the church family has a parent to sit with on Sunday morning. Not every single adult knows what it is like to be an intricate part of a family. The church cannot assume that because grandfather was a deacon, the son will be a deacon and the grandson, in time, will share the honor. A few years ago, the St. Charles Avenue Baptist Church in New Orleans recognized several families who had supported the local congregation through three generations. Fortunate are those church families and extended families who have "something going for themselves." These families deserve credit and recognition.

The church cannot assume, though, that relationships are of high quality even when persons of the extended family network are together in one church family. It is possible for extended families to sit in Sunday morning worship and not see each other during the rest of the week. The church has an opportunity to help extended family systems remain operative, while furnishing simulated networks for those nuclear families who are isolated and detached with their own natural extended family system.

The church cannot lose its identity as a "family"—Christ's family. There are churches and church-related organizations who have, consciously or unconsciously, created a ministry to "adults only." They are not openly stating a policy of "No Children Allowed" as the private apartment landlords and city planners are doing, but the intuitive feeling is there—no children allowed. No youth allowed either, unless they can stretch their abilities and function on the adult level.

Jesus reached out to a little child, placed that child in the midst of the disciples, and said: "Whoever receives one such child in my name receives me; but whoever causes one of these little ones who believe in me to sin, it would be better for him to have a great millstone fastened round his neck and to be drowned in the depth of the sea" (Matt. 18:5-6, RSV).

The church that loses sight of the children and youth who are in their midst are warned of severe outcomes. Even those who do not believe in Jesus' admonishment to the disciples know that the children of tomorrow are important. Biologically speaking, the species that does not reproduce its own, will become extinct. Organically, the seed that is not placed in a nurturing context does not yield fruit in the next season. Economically, the organization that does not maintain itself will fold. More specifically, the family of faith that loses its next generation will grow old and die away.

The church, as family, has a future as it ministers to the next generation. Will the ministry be intentionally intergenerational? Will extended family groups be a step in the right direction? The concept of combining all ages is not new or unique with Christians. The concept and pattern is old.

The newness of the concept comes merely in transforming the modes and techniques into programs and models that are usable in the contemporary fellowship of faith.

Tasks of the Extended Family

The ultimate task of the extended family group is like the major task of any other small group within the family of faith—"to build up the church, the body of Christ."

Groups, like persons, have different goals to which their ministry is directed. To fulfill their goals, groups must decide upon their tasks. When the goals and tasks are defined, people supply the forms with life and vitality.

In Ephesians 4:7-16, Paul speaks about the diversity of gifts that are given to members of God's family. In group life, these gifts are manifested *through* people *to* people. The gifts are used for the good of the group. The family of God, as a group—big or small, reaches inward to minister to its own members but also reaches outward to minister to those who are not members.

The extended family group seeks to be a smaller model of the family of God—living out the teachings of Jesus and building upon the framework of the early Christian fellowships. The tasks that the extended family assume are few, but they are intended to blend, enhance, and supplement the work of the church as it ministers in a contemporary world.

(1) The task of the extended family is to *provide an opportunity for nuclear families to become a part of a bigger, broader family system.*

The extended family exists solely because someone wants it! Nuclear families are turning to the church for support and encouragement. The "great distances" which separate nuclear families from their natural extended families are physical distances (number of miles) and functional distances (breakdown of relationships and interaction).

The church has an opportunity, even a duty and responsibility, to open its structural arms to the isolated family units who are seeking others to share life. When an entire family says, "We want to be adopted," the family of faith cannot turn its back. Neither can an entire congregation be expected to wholeheartedly say, "We'll care for you and love you." Whole congregations do not operate on that intimate, personal basis. What usually happens when a family makes a plea to the church family is that a few individuals or several family units respond. The extended family concept is an attempt to provide a family network which is bigger than a nuclear family unit and smaller than an entire congregation.

(2) The task of the extended family is to *provide a family for individuals whose immediate family is fragmented.*

Fragmentation in families is brought about by divorce and death. Fragmentation is also brought about by differences in life-styles and value choices. The extended family, like the church, ministers to families, and it also ministers to parts of families. Teenagers may choose to join the extended family group out of a need that other family members do not share. A husband, or wife, or single adult, might participate without other family members. Most often, in past groups, there are children who become a part of the extended family because parents are engaged in other church responsibilities or because the parents are not interested in "more family."

In working with family systems, there is evidence that when one person becomes a part of a group, either for enrichment or therapy purposes, the change that takes place in the life of that individual has an effect on other family

members as well. Although the ideal would be to have total
family participation in order that all members could share
the experience and take the experience back to their home
setting for evaluation and debriefing, reality says that is not
always possible. Therefore, the task of the extended family
is to provide for the "parts of immediate families."

(3) The task of the extended family is to *build a bridge
between the generations.*

Bridges are significant objects in our world. Bridges connect two bodies of water or areas of land. Bridges connect
two parts of a song. Bridges connect two teeth. Bridges in
the extended family connect the generations—the different
age groups.

The need for bridge-building groups within the church
has not always existed. Age segregation began a noticeable
appearance in about the nineteenth century, first among
the urban middle-class Americans. Children of middle-class
families were entering and leaving schools at specified ages
and for specified periods of time. Patterns of transition from
one age to another were being recognized and studied. The
stages of childhood were delineated. Then the study of ado-
lescence came along. Distinct stages of life and orderly pro-
gression from one age to another began to dictate the formation of groups and classes. In the twentieth century, the
adult stages of life began to be divided along the lines of
age and roles.

As the state and church institutions gradually took over
the functions that had previously lodged in the family, there
was even greater conformity to timing sequences. Sunday
Schools became divided not only by sex, but by age. The
schools became stricter on age requirements for first-graders.
Compulsory school attendance was set at a definite age. The
labor laws began to place age restrictions on child labor
and on adult retirement.

The mass media widen the gaps by gearing programs and advertising to certain age groups and role functions of the viewers. Products are now designed for the teenagers only, for housewives only, for the man of the house, and for children only—occasionally the "family only" phrase is seen.

The subtle and not-so-subtle influences of society are spreading apart the generations. The "widening" trend has now become an object of concern and the swing is toward "bridging the gap." Thus, the extended family is in the bridge-building business.

The intergenerational mixture of this specific group means that all ages are represented. The five age groupings that are most descriptive are: children, youth, young adults, median adults, and older adults. Persons from each of the five age groupings are desired in an intergenerational combination, such as extended family. Just children and the older adults are not enough. Just youth and median adults are not enough. Extended families need some of each age.

The extended family is a group that continually seeks to build new bridges for making the interaction between generations happen. New games, new techniques, new activities—old games, old techniques, old activities—all resources that constitute bridge-building materials are the resources for extended family groups.

(4) The task of the extended family is to *find a new grandfather for the five-year-old and a grandson for the seventy-year-old.*

The extended family group is like a clearing house or a data bank that makes exchanges and match-ups. In this technological world where one can find a date, a new husband or wife, a new child, a new house, or a new kidney by programming information into a computer and waiting for answers, the extended family becomes somewhat like a manually-operated computer.

When our own preschool boy and one of his friends needed adults to sit with them during morning worship, the extended family group was the place where the request was made. People responded and out of the exchange came relationships that are so priceless that only time will be able to calculate the true value.

During one of the weeks at a large denominational assembly, ten youth needed a group to call their own. They were young people who had come to the assembly of three thousand persons to participate in a special "speaker's tournament." These youth usually came without other members of their local church group. They came with parents or adult chaperons. This meant they were alone on the assembly campus grounds and sometimes did not feel a part of the other large groups of youth. The "Second Family" group at the assembly was a group that needed them, invited them to join and provided them with an intimate, easy-to-fit-in group. The match-up was perfect for these youth—and for the children and adults who needed and wanted them.

The extended family group is in the business of matching up people. This task is taken seriously. Unfortunately, eight weeks or thirteen weeks or half a year is not much time to work on building these relationships. When the weeks are considered as hours that are actually spent together in the extended family group, the time is minimal—eight hours, fifteen hours, twenty-six hours. The matching up can be done within those few hours, but there must be a mutual feeling, a good "vibration," a meeting of needs that makes the few weeks and hours of maximum importance. The task of the extended family is to provide a fertile, nurturant atmosphere for relationship building in order to get the match-up off to a good start.

(5) The task of the extended family is to *provide a supportive group atmosphere for . . . personal growth, observing*

other family members from new perspectives, and
*practicing new behaviors that will enhance family liv-
ing.*

"I have grown in my ability to relate, to show concern,
to speak to other ages, and understand my own leadership
abilities," said one extended family member.

It is nice to think that we never stop growing. Being in
new kinds of groups and doing new kinds of activities are
refreshing changes for some members of the church family.
Growth that is stimulated by newness of environment and
newness of relationships is important to adults and children
alike. Educators tell us that the best preparation for young
children as they come to school is to have given the child
a good background of experiences. Building blocks for academic life are gained by being with people, establishing
relationships, exploring new territories, being involved in
numerous activities. These building blocks are then trans-
formed into content and knowledge. If new settings and
new relationships are important to children, they are equally
important to youth and adults.

Growth in a special atmosphere can be rapid. Bacteria
that enters a host organism, like our human bodies, can mul-
tiply at a rate which is almost unbelievable. One germ can
become over 500 trillion germs in twelve hours if the atmosphere is good. Growth is not that rapid for us in extended
family groups, but growth can be achieved in a few months.
People can testify to what has happened to them.

"I got to know a side of my father and mother that I
didn't know. I was pleased." (Words of a teenage girl.)

Have you ever viewed your house or town from a plane
from a tree house, from a house high on a hill. The world
moves and takes on patterns that are never obvious when
one is below in that setting. We get a different perspective
of the ordinary.

Too often we fail to look at ourselves and our loved ones

from different perspectives. Perhaps you have had a child say to you, "I didn't know you could do that!" It is an interesting sensation to know that you have been observed in a new light. The first time our son noticed that I could play softball was at a Labor Day picnic at the church. He came running up to me on first base, yelling, "You hit the ball. I didn't know you could play ball." He had never seen me play sandlot ball. As he grew older, he saw me from the light of his own ability as a ball player and recognized me as one who really couldn't "play ball"—I just played at it.

People, like the teenager who made the statement above concerning her father and mother, are sometimes surprised when they learn something new about family members. Just when our levels of intimacy seem deep, we see another facet of our loved ones. Although this "new knowing" keeps marriages and family life alive, it may cause negative and positive movements in the family. The mother who observes her son smoking a cigarette for the first time might not perceive this new knowing as positive. On the other hand, the father who watches his daughter run seven miles across the countryside with a bunch of afternoon joggers might perceive of the new knowing as a high event.

The new learning that can take place in the extended family is best utilized if it is gained in a supportive atmosphere. The goal and task of the extended family is to keep the group warm and open in order that new knowledge about one another can be used in helpful ways.

"I tried a new way of communicating that I would never have tried at home with my family," said a mother.

Families are lacking in communication and relationship-building skills and techniques. We are not talking to one another. We are not trying new ways of relating.

Families talk when crises hit! They are made to confront each other and the situation. Often they are assisted by pastors, counselors, or social service agencies. After the bad scenes are over, attempts to keep the channels open are sabotaged by busy schedules, absences from each other, and several hundred other legitimate reasons.

Many families just "feel silly" trying a new technique or a new method of behaving when they are alone in the house. They are embarrassed. They read the "how to" books, but they are afraid to try the suggestions given at the end of the chapter.

The extended family group offers persons a group atmosphere that welcomes new attempts. Making errors and mistakes in the supportive atmosphere of a loving family group is different from making mistakes in a group that criticizes, jumps on your back, and offers harsh judgments. The extended family provides a specific time for attempting new things. The experiential, doing-rather-than-talking approach to learning, allows more opportunities for group members to try on new behaviors and to act in new ways. Persons in extended family groups are encouraged to "try."

Is there a carry-over from learning in the extended family to the home situation of members? Although there has been no special study of this question, testimonies from participants indicate some positive carry-over—activities and situations that happened within the group did give them new tools for relating at home. One parent said, "We saw our children in a different light and this helped relationships at home."

(6) The task of the extended family is to *become one big happy family by working together.*

When one looks in a camera viewer and sees the circle where all is a blurr, there is an adjustment which can be made which brings the subject into clearer focus. In the extended family the focus is adjusted more toward cooperation rather than toward competition.

In 1 Peter 3:8, the admonition is given to the early Christians to "be like one big happy family, full of sympathy toward each other, loving one another with tender hearts and humble minds." That admonition fits well into the family life of the twentieth century. It suggests that families become involved in the physical and mental and emotional world of each other.

In the extended family, working together is done by becoming involved in projects that require the help of all the members. What kind of "bigger-than-all-of-us" projects can extended families have to get the members working side by side?

- The extended family can set a goal which involves everyone—a progressive dinner was the final project of one Second Family group.

- Another extended family group used their weekend retreat to prepare for a Sunday evening worship for the entire congregation. The group reached beyond itself into the church family.

- The extended family group can reach beyond itself and the local church family into the community at large by becoming involved with social action projects.

In the extended family, working together on decisions means "I win and you win." To come to a consensus among the members means everyone may have to give some ground in order for everyone to feel good about the final decision. The ability to share opinions is respected even down to the youngest member.

In the extended family, problems and conflicts are kept out in the open. Family feuding is a joke among clans and extended family groups; but if complaints and dissatisfactions are kept on the table at all times, the working together comes easier and the feuding is avoided.

Even though the focus adjustment is toward cooperation, is there a time when competition helps the family work together? Yes, competitiveness can make a team out of individual players. Positive, low-keyed techniques can create a group spirit.

At one of the Baptist conference centers, the extended family group was formed from forty-five individuals who came from many different communities. One or two persons knew each other prior to the week of being together, but mostly the members were strangers—new faces, new personalities. Many small groups were meeting simultaneously during that week. The extended family was one group among the many.

The intergenerational group gave the outward appearance of being an extended family, but the relationships were far from resembling those of a close-knit family group. Because the group would only meet for six days, three hours per day, extra effort was spent on building relationships—quickly. Face-to-face interaction, use of first names, and sharing of personal stories and feelings were just a few techniques used at the first sessions.

Extra effort was also spent on building the forty-five individuals into a distinct group on the assembly campus. To make the individuals become a team—quickly, subtle competitive techniques were used. Phrases like "Our family group does such-and-such" or "The extended family looks like . . ." were repeated. The participants were asked to make comparisons of the extended family group to other groups in which they had been members.

The team-building and relationship-building efforts were successful. Family members expressed appreciation for the extended family experience during an evaluation period. One female participant shared her feelings by telling of a situation that had happened after the third day of being together as a group.

The lady, a pastor's wife, said she was always called by her title, Mrs. _____, by the youth and children in her local church family. She also related that she had been to the conference center many times before and had been a part of many kinds of learning groups. During this particular week, however, something new happened. While walking across the conference center campus, she heard someone calling her first name. When she turned around to respond, she discovered that a teenager, standing some far distance off, was waving and yelling her name. The youth, who knew few of the other thousands of people on the conference center grounds, was calling out just to say, "I know you." The older woman marveled that she enjoyed being called by her first name—by a teenager! She also marveled at the delightful feeling of being recognized by another person who was a member of her "group." The feeling of belonging to a special group was strengthened by the added factor of recognition and intimacy from the teenager.

The competitiveness that brought this extended family together into a "oneness" was a positive factor.

3
Forming the Extended Family:
Calling Forth Commitments

Memory is one of the greatest sources of human happiness and human suffering. If we want to celebrate our lives in the present, we cannot cut off ourselves from our past. We are instead, invited to look at our history as the sequence of events that brought us where we are now and that help us to understand what it means to be here at this moment in this world.

Henri J. M. Nouwen

The extended family group that formed within the Immanuel Baptist Church in 1974 was the final stage of development for a concept that had been growing within people for quite some time. Before the final product came the search. Before the searching came an awareness of a need. Before the awareness of a need came the patterns for living and relating that made an extended family important to our lives. The formation of the extended family did not come from *nothing—nothing comes from nothing.* The forming of an extended family began a long time ago . . . .

. . . in the late summer of 1963, John and I loaded up our furniture into the rented one-way moving van—all, that is, except the old metal coil bedsprings. They could not be fitted into, on top of, or behind the van. Leaving the bedsprings in the custody of my dad and mother who had come to help us pack, we left Missouri. We left the background of our origins—our folks, our homestate, our mid-west way of life.

The leaving had no great significance at that time. We were a young couple—married five years, and we were off to New Orleans where John would continue his education at the Baptist seminary. A job was waiting at the St. Charles Avenue Baptist Church for both of us—John would be youth director and I would be the pastor's secretary. We had an apartment on the seminary campus and an invitation to Saturday dinner with the pastor and his family. We had a lot going and a lot to do.

In my mind, I can still see the long bridge that crosses Lake Pontchartrain and brings one into the "City That Care Forgot." The blue of the water, the mile markers on the long bridge, and the first view of the city skyline will always be etched in my memory. That bridge, through the years, has become the symbol of leaving behind the family network of relatives and kin and the beginning of the search for other persons who would be "family."

The two people who drove across the Pontchartrain Bridge with all their material possessions did not leave the city as the same people. Life in New Orleans saw a time of change and growth.

In the years between 1963 and 1966, many experiences brought new people into our lives—people who have become significant. Some of these persons came from the seminary community and some from the church congregation. Out of the numerous groups of students with whom we met, talked, worked, and shared, two couples joined with us to form into a group like no other group we had experienced. This community of peers was accompanied by two preschool children, the daughters of one of the couples. The last year of those days in New Orleans found this small group taking on a dynamic that is known to few groups. Because of the power of small group process and the additional power that is furnished to people who are at one in the faith in Jesus, the group began to exemplify the fruits of the spirit that Paul speaks of in his writings. The group members began to give and receive love, acceptance, forgiveness, joy, peace, and patience. What the six of us were experiencing was very much what all of us thought "church" must be. Out of respect for our tradition of what the local church should be, none of us felt comfortable in saying, "We are the church." All of us spoke of our feelings and our frustration that we could not conceive of ourselves as church. We knew our experience was what should, ought, and could happen with a group of believers; yet we also knew that the church is more than a peer group of adults meeting together in Jesus' name. Church was more. Church was all ages. Church was many ministries. Our experience in the group told us, however, that we "knew" what it was to be the church.

Alongside the growth of our peer-group relationships, we were developing family bonds with our pastor, his wife, and their three children. Much time was spent together. Saturday night was always hamburger night at their house with an open invitation for us to join them. When important people came to visit their home, we were invited to meet the guests and share in the fellowship. When the children needed someone to stay at the house during absences by their parents, we were available to spend nights.

The ease with which our lives became entangled is still a mystery. We needed and they gave; they gave, and we accepted; they needed and we responded. It all worked so naturally. Love and mutual support grew and our community of people included peers and family of all ages. Our immediate family also grew during those years in New Orleans. When we left to move to Nashville, Tennessee, in October of 1966, we left with a daughter—Melissa.

With our "peer family" separated by the graduation of
the husbands—with our "extended family" left behind in
New Orleans, with all our relatives scattered in Pennsylva-
nia, Missouri, and Louisiana, we were three people alone
in the new city. Because our lives had been influenced by
the communities and family of our past, we began to consciously seek out persons to be sharers of life. We invited
persons to our home and said, "We need a group." We began
to reveal our lives in hopes that others would pick up on
the sharing and, in turn, feel comfortable in revealing themselves. We were searching but we did not have an identifiable term for that which we needed. We had not fully realized that we had lost "community" and "family." We just
knew that life had lost something which had been important!

Involvements with new friends, our church, and our work
brought busy days. Our lives were quickly developing into
patterns that resembled the "model family."

In 1969, Jud was born and we delighted in having the
two children in our lives. Along with the delight came the
usual frustrations, anxiety, and turmoil involved with small
children—fever, earaches, toilet training—tears mixed with
smiles.

The dissatisfaction with our sense of community and our
extended family situation began to be more clearly focused
in the early 1970s. We realized that we were not alone in
some of our frustrations. Other people were expressing the
desire to try new forms of community. The extreme forms
were shaping into communal living with groups of people
contracting and banding together into "families" and "communities." These people were leaving jobs, selling their resi-
dences and property, and pooling their physical, financial,
and emotional resources.

On Labor Day, 1970, a small group of persons in Nashville
met to discuss the possibility of forming a "house church."

We were invited to attend that initial meeting. The people in that group including several couples who were students or teachers in the academic community, several couples with young children, and several single adults. Curiosity brought most of us to the meeting. Curiosity got us there, but our mutual experience had been that of disappointment with past religious education forms, a need for a support group who were immediately available, and a desire to give more to other persons than most of our relationships demanded from us. The group struggled through several months of planning and finally became an incorporated nonprofit organization known as "Covenant Community."

For two and one-half years our family was an active part of what we called "little church." Our involvement in our "big church" continued and between the two churches we attempted to meet the needs that were ever present in our lives—community and extended family.

Covenant Community made a difference in our lives. We worked hard to become all that a church could be through worship, Bible study, education, outreach, and ministry in social action areas. We met regularly and on special occasions. We developed a ministry to transient youth through a house known as "Affirmation House." We took our lives together seriously. We wanted to develop a community and yet maintain our separate family units. We struggled with finding new forms that would be effective. We found that worship together with the children in our midst was rewarding, but different. One of those unforgetable worship experiences centered around our partaking of the bread and juice during a service of communion. The children were seated in the middle of the group during the worship. When the closing circle was being formed, one father reached down to pick up his toddler. As we stood and drew close, we sang a song and bowed our heads for the benediction. In the midst of the silence and meditation, a tremendous "burp" issued forth from the toddler. The moment of seriousness was interrupted and rather than having a closing of peace and benediction, we concluded with joyous laughter and hugging. Where else but in a small family-like group could worship be so informal and spontaneous and be benedicted with a burp!

Within those months of planning and trying new patterns of group-building, worship forms, and innovative approaches to educating ourselves and the children, we discovered that no easy answers were to be found in the "little church." Likewise, there were numerous problems connected with the "big church."

In the mid 1970s, many small groups of people were banding together both within and without the organized church. Some groups were trying to become "house churches." Others, called tape groups, listened to cassette-taped messages and then discussed the material. Still others were prayer groups who met to pray and support each other. Small groups were springing up everywhere. As a result, the large, organized churches began suffering in some program areas. People were staying away from the church in order to have their needs met in the outside groups.

In 1973, our family was faced with a choice. We could not physically remain active in two churches. Our lives and the lives of our children were being pulled, and we were tired. Our investments in the "big church" were great and we decided that we must release our involvement in our "house church." The choice did not come without struggle and loss.

But we had learned something. We had been provided with new experiences. We knew that our needs for community and extended family would probably always be a source of discontentment. We had realized that we must actively seek out and provide for ourselves those things which we lacked. With God's guidance and using the ideas that were being created by his divine providence, we would continue to do what we could to find our extended family within the "big church." The active seeking led to the search for a "Second Family" group in the fall and winter of 1973.

The birth of the extended family concept came from something—nothing comes from nothing! The birth came about because of our past relationships, our experiences at community-building—positive and negative, our hurts and joys, our gains and losses, our aloneness and our togetherness. We were pulling something together during the years. We were nurturing an idea. We were not alone for others were learning, too. Others were willing to try something new based on experiences that had happened to them.

The coming together—the conception—had happened. Our personal need and our desire to do something based on what we knew to do had come together. In God's family we could find extended family who shared our faith. It would be our shared faith in Jesus that brought us together. From our commitment to Jesus as our brother and God as our father, we could move forward to other commitments within God's family.

The birth of the extended family model took place when specific needs and basic assumptions of learning were sufficiently developed. Nothing comes from nothing . . . .

All Ages in One Big Family

The extended family model is formed around the general assumption that persons of all ages will interact together in a family-like context. These assumptions can be broken down into three areas: (1) interaction between the ages (2) distribution of all ages, and (3) structuring of the group. Participants in extended family groups, who have shared their comments and suggestions after each experience, provided insight into which of our basic assumptions were most valuable and unique. Their comments are sprinkled through the chapter.

Interaction Between the Ages

"I liked the opportunity to interact with persons of all ages."

How would you define the difference between *being in the presence* of people who represent several generations of life and *interacting with people* who represent several generations of life? There is a distinct difference in the *being with* and *interacting with* and it is that difference which makes extended family experiences unique from many other intergenerational events.

In designing a setting or environment for the extended family group, intentional consideration is given to the distances between people. One kind of distance is physical—the linear distance between persons. In the church there are many opportunities for people of all ages to be close—physically. We worship together. We eat together. We fellowship after church. We sit together at the weekly baseball game. We roller-skate beside each other at the activities building. These intergenerational events bring persons together in a context for being with one another.

How much interaction takes place at the intergenerational events you attend? Do you find yourself always sitting with the same few people? Do you notice new faces in the crowd and wonder who these persons are? Do you strike up conversations with people you do not know very well?

The functional distance between people is the second distance which is important in designing the setting for the extended family group. This distance factor involves the ability to be in contact with others. This distance deals with interaction with and between individuals.

To shorten the functional distance between individuals it is usually necessary to provide a "way" that this can happen. Rather than instruct persons in the extended family to "Sit down and find out something new about each other," we assist the get-acquainted process by putting them in a double circle of persons and giving them a specific topic to discuss within a specific time limit. To ask persons to touch each other usually brings a negative response, but suggesting they play a contact game is much less threatening.

Interaction is the objective behind activities that allow people of all ages to sit with knees touching knees doing mirror/reflection actions, or molding clay in small groups, or planning refreshments for the next session. To make contact with one another is the underlying purpose for finding games, activities, music, and worship that all persons can participate in regardless of age.

To allow maximum time for personal interaction avoid activities such as lectures, long stories or readings, movies (unless interaction is a part of the debriefing), and other formal teaching techniques which place one or two persons as the actors and the remainder of the family as spectators.

Distribution of Ages

"The vitality of the young, the experience of the old. You begin to get a perspective of wholeness."

To intentionally start picking people from certain age brackets makes designing an extended family experience sound like we are playing a game where we have to choose ten marbles of either blue, green, yellow, or red. Being choosy or manipulative is not the purpose of specifying that certain numbers of people be represented within a range of ages. The goal is to combine family units that provide a distribution from young to old. The isolation of a certain age is what often happens in real life. In extended family, an effort is made to form a group where there is some of everyone.

Our first attempts at forming extended family groups in the church provided insight into why a good distribution of ages is necessary. In the first "Second Family" the total number of participants stayed around the forty mark. The initial planning for the group was thoroughly worked out. Persons to fill each age group were sought out and personally contacted. Our worksheet looked like this:

Age group	Desired number of persons	Participants
Preschool	2	(names)
Children	8	
Youth	8	
Young Adults	5	
Median Adults	10	
Older Adults	7	

The wide distribution of ages, plus having twenty to twenty-five adults and older youth gave a solid basis. There were enough adults to carry the load of the planning and there were enough children and youth to make the group lively and active.

In the second formation of an extended family group, the children outnumbered the adults. Some of the children were participating without their parents. This created a situation where more of the major planning fell upon the fewer number of adults in the group. The evaluations from this experience reemphasized the need for an even distribution of ages. Groups that have all youth and children with no adults or all adults with no younger generations represented are self-defeating formations for an extended family group.

"The Pied Piper"

Purpose: To focus on the importance of having all ages represented in the extended family group by stating what would be missed if each age grouping was not present.

Supplies needed: A storyteller and a piper.

Process: Be prepared to tell the story of the Pied Piper of Hamelin. A detailed story can be found in an encyclopedia or in literature books. Briefly, the account of the mythical character is as follows: The German town of Hamelin (according to legend) was infested with rats. The Mayor of the town offered a large money reward to anyone who could rid the city of the rats. One day a man dressed in a suit of many colors walked through the town piping on his pipe. The rats came out of their hiding place and followed him. He led them into the nearby river and all the rats drowned. When the piper went to the mayor for his reward, he was refused the money. The piper was very displeased. Taking his pipe, he again walked through the streets. He piped a magical melody that charmed all the children of the village. They followed him through the streets and into a cave outside the city. The children were never seen again.

Set the scene for the storytelling, by asking the family to sit in a large circle. The storyteller will invite all the children, twelve years and younger, to come sit on the floor in the center. Begin by telling the story of the legendary Pied Piper. Have a piper, who has been secured earlier, sit in the circle, too. When the story is finished, the piper will rise from his or her chair, pipe a melody on a song flute or recorder, and motion the children to follow. After leading the children around the inside of the circle, the piper will again direct them to sit in the middle of the circle. The storyteller will tell the children: This time you are to pretend you are in an invisible cave. No adults and youth can see you. You are to be silent, so no one will know where you are. (Give the directions to the children using a very mysterious, low voice.)

After the children are silent in their invisible (but not invisible) cave, turn to the youth and adults and say: The children are gone. We have no children in our group. Do you miss them? What do you miss about the children? (Allow time for the adults and youth to name off qualities which they miss when children are absent.)

Now, ask the youth to join the children in the invisible cave. Again, give the children and youth instructions to sit very quietly. Ask the adults: With the youth gone, too; what do you miss about them. What do the youth add which is lacking now? (Allow time for answers.)

Finally, direct questions to the youth and children who have been silently listening. Ask: Children and youth, you are alone in the cave. All the grown-up people are away. What do you miss about mothers and daddies and grandparents? What do you miss when the adults are not with you? (Wait for answers.)

End the activity by reminding the members of the family that everyone is important. Every age is important. One person in an extended family said it well: "The vitality of the young, the experience of the old. You begin to get a perspective of wholeness."

Structuring of Group Size

"I like the feeling of gathering with a family group week after week to play and worship together. A church could have several of these groups going all the time."

How many people shall we have in our extended family? In designing a "simulated" extended family there is some leeway in how many will be in a group. Do not, however, confuse purposeful structuring of a group for size to mean that a group becomes "closed." The extended family experiences do have a way of settling in, that is, certain people keep coming back; but there is always room for an occasional "visiting cousin" or the "new arrival."

The structuring of the extended family's size is an intentional attempt to make the group workable. The factors that need to be considered are the type of activities and available meeting space.

Large group—small groups.—Part of the activities in the extended family are built for small groups of five to eight people. The small group concept provides more opportunities for individual sharing and interaction. Each session should include some activity for small group work.

Extended family experiences are designed for the immediate family members to be in the same large group and yet not be with one another every minute. When the facilitator of an activity gives instructions for small family groups to form, the participants learn to group themselves with a diversity of ages—some children, one or two youth, a few adults of all ages. Usually individual members of a nuclear family are asked to work in different groups. There are occasions when the younger children need to stay with a parent or older sibling because of security needs. That is understood and they are accommodated. The extended family members learn this method of grouping by having it stressed over and over, if necessary, by the persons leading the sessions. Usually after several weeks in the extended family experience, the members in the group know how to "eyeball" a forming group and place themselves where needed to achieve a family-like mixture.

Since the purpose of the extended family is to experience all ages together, part of the activities are done in one large group. The movement from the large group into small groups and back to the large group is flexible, but necessary. The small groups facilitate getting acquainted on a more one-to-one level and the large group helps the family to visualize the extended family in its entirety.

Availability of meeting space.—The extended family needs ample space. The small groups need to be visible to one another. Visibility is the key. One family member said, "When I can *see* other groups my interest and motivation are higher."

Select a room in which tables or work areas can be used by small groups when necessary and then used by the large group. A fellowship hall, recreation area, or large classroom are good places. Some groups have used the out-of-doors when the weather permitted or when activities required it.

What size group is best? The most workable size for your group might come through trial and error. Some extended families feel forty is a good number. For a weekend retreat with lots of space and a small amount of time, a group of seventy-five to eighty has proved successful. With a large number of persons, 100-150 or over, three or four extended family groups could be formed with thirty-five to forty-five in each group. The activities could be similar but different meeting rooms should be provided.

"The Family Portrait"

Purpose: To behold the extended family in all its sizes, shapes, ages, and combinations.

Process: This activity will take a large room with open space. Ask the group to stand in a large circle. Each movement of people organizes clockwise around the circle. For instance, in the formation of the circle by persons' size, the smallest will be standing between 12:00 and 1:00. Moving around the circle clockwise, the tallest will be standing between 11:00 and 12:00. After each circle formation, allow adequate time for persons to "behold" or "see" the group in this way. Here are some suggested circle formations.

1. By first name alphabetically
2. By birthdays—months and days
3. By size—from shortest to tallest
4. By age—from youngest to oldest

Another way of "seeing" an extended family is through geographical locations. Change the room into an imaginary map of the United States. Identify north, south, east, and west and identify two or three major landmarks to help persons get their bearings (like Mississippi River, Rocky Mountains, Great Lakes). Then ask persons to "move" to the following areas. Allow time for discussion at each "station."

1. The place where you were born
2. The place where one of your parents was born
3. The place you would like to visit
4. A place where a good friend or relative lives

Through these "movements" of people you will "see" other extended family members in new relationships. One person described it as one of his most meaningful church experiences: "It was as if I was seeing our church family for the first time. It was beautiful!"

Building a Committed Extended Family

How much can be expected of members of an extended family group? Will they attend regularly? Will they participate in the activities? Will family members commit themselves to the group? How do we talk about contracts and covenanting together?

As members of God's family we should never be embarrassed or ashamed of using contracts and covenants. Ours is a heritage of committed followers to God's covenant. We have had covenants modeled for us throughout biblical history. We are participants in a covenant relationship with God and with other Christians. We are bound together by our commitments.

In building extended families we can learn from the process of contracting and committing. The following diagram shows the process:

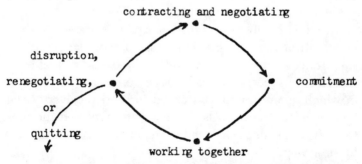

Using the diagram, we can follow the process of committing in the extended family model.

Contracting and Negotiating. At the very first contact, potential members are given the approximate times, dates, and purposes of the extended family group. There will be a certain amount of negotiating that can be done about the length of sessions, special meeting times, and similar concerns after the initial commitments to join have been made. The first session is the time for firming up the contract and finalizing any last minute negotiations.

Shared leadership, involvement through regular attendance, and active participation are three major portions of the contracting agenda. Children and youth are encouraged to speak and ask questions if they do not understand what is being agreed upon. The negotiating and contracting need not be heavy and serious. Let there be confusion, laughter, talking, and questioning. Use a big sheet of newsprint with some expectations written down. Use calendar sheets designating the months and weeks with space for persons to volunteer their leadership for these weeks. Keep the contracting process informal and light.

Commitments. The commitments are not written in black ink on parchment, nor are they made by the exchange of blood. There is informality and casualness, yet there needs to be a feeling that we are either going to do it or we are not. The commitment can make the difference.

Extended family groups from our past have been in three major settings: in the local church, as a part of a large national conference center program, and as a weekend retreat experience. The success stories have come out of those groups in which commitment was called for and received. In all these settings the persons who gave and received the most from the experience were those who made that commitment to the group.

Working Together. I wish there was some way to share the joy of being in an extended family group. Words cannot describe what happens—photos that are better than a thousand words do not tell the whole story—extended family groups must be experienced. The best way the model can be shared is by doing some of it. Your first attempts must be a dedicated effort to "make it work by working together." The more times members participate in extended family groups the more experienced they become. Working together again and again leads into new ideas and new hopes for what the group can be. The joint endeavor will include rejoicing in the successes and learning from the failures. After some weekly sessions, the members learn to say, "Let's do it again" or "Let's don't do that again." Experience and evaluation become the teachers.

Disruption, Renegotiating, or Quitting. Social systems, big or small, end. The length of time that it takes depends upon the system. The family is a good example of a large system that gives the impression of ending in the future years of our lifetime. However, if we look backward into history, we find hope that the family system has a pattern of changing—not ending.

In a group as small as the extended family, it is possible to plan for the contract cycle to have an ending. Disruption may come before the designated ending and occasionally, members may quit; but if the time is planned out intentionally, there will be less chance of that happening. The ending and beginning are important to the extended family contract. With positive endings come the opportunities for renegotiating—new beginnings.

The next three sections suggest the use of three major contractual items: (1) short-term study concept, (2) shared leadership concept, and (3) active-participation concept.

Beginning and Ending: Short-Term Study Concept

"Periodic evaluation and regrouping is often difficult but necessary."

The extended family group is not designed to continue indefinitely. Many classes and fellowship groups within the church have been in existence for years and years. These are "on-going" groups. The extended family group falls into the category of "short-term study groups." There is a specific length of time in which the group will be together with a particular purpose.

When the model for an extended family was being formed, the short-term group concept seemed most workable. People are busy. Family schedules get crowded quickly. Common sense said that families could not promise an hour and a half a week for a year or two, but they would commit themselves to one night a week for three months. The added plus in placing the extended family group into the Sunday night or Wednesday night program of the church is that these nights are already cleared on many family calendars.

If the commonsense reasons for designing the extended family group as a short-term group were not sufficient, there is still the theoretical reason. People, if not given an opportunity to stop participation in a group, will in time, find a reason.

Lessons have been learned from previous extended family group experiences. The quoted comments from past participants provide insights into what families feel about joining and attending the extended family sessions.

"*Do it! Like we did it!*" This remark is just too good to be excluded! The time, the activities—everything was right. A guess would be that this person was "ready" for such a group. In the beginning, look for people who are ready! If people have expressed an interest in the extended family idea, contact these persons first and find out how much interest they have. Ask if they would be available to help form the core group and ask what period of time is clear for them to give to the effort. After three or four families agree to commit themselves for the same eight weeks, or three months, or whatever length of time seems best, this will provide a nucleus of committed members.

"I'm out of town one Sunday night each month." Some families are very aware of their schedule because they have fixed responsibilities that must be given priority. In one family, the dad was a salesman who traveled and had to leave for his territory on a Sunday night. Other families faced similar scheduling problems but they were willing to declare what nights or sessions they could come and, then, committed themselves to attend. Knowing when people can come is helpful. Knowing when people plan to be absent is equally helpful.

"A couple of nights I had rather stayed home, but. . . ." The commitment to come and participate is what makes people put out the extra effort to attend a group. When every night of the week is filled with activities, when a ball game is being played by your favorite team, when the topic just does not sound all that interesting, that is when the commitment makes the difference. The person who made the above statement spoke encouragingly because the whole statement should read: "A couple of nights I had rather stayed home, but after I came, it was well worth coming." When the extended family experience is good, then the extra effort is worth the expenditure. Calling for commitments to begin and end helps members be responsible for their attendance.

"I guess it's better to stop on a good note." Any public relations expert would echo the sentiments expressed by this participant. "Leave them laughing!" and "Make them want to come back for more!" are enticements for the next event. When the extended family experience ends, there will be mixtures of sadness and relief. That is natural. That is good. That is why beginning and ending is intentional and built into the design.

"Three months is not long enough." With each ending there is the opportunity for a new beginning for those per-

sons who want to continue in such an intergenerational group. The new beginning is a way of opening up the group to new members, to fresh insights, to new relationships. The opening-up process is a way of saying we want to stay alive. The extended family group will not want to become cliquish and with each stopping and starting the chance of one "group" of persons becoming too tied in with one another is reduced.

Remember this! Define the time elements when the extended family group is still in the preplanning stages. Be mindful of the season, the weather, the outside activities of families, the church's schedule, and the purpose for the group. Then proceed. In the first session, spell out the contract of time involvements, negotiate where necessary, and seek commitments.

Sometimes a Leader: Shared Leadership Concept

"In sharing leadership we are all prompted to give something of ourselves. All were encouraged to give."

If we define leadership as the actions on the part of an extended family member that influence the group toward setting and achieving certain goals, then potentially each member of the group may play a role in the group's leadership. The phrase "shared leadership" simply means all members can be leaders. The amount and degree of leadership varies with one's abilities and with the task.

In the definition of leadership, the phrase "actions on the part of the extended family member that influence the group" is commonly recognized as one's expertise. An expert is one whose actions can be influential. We often think of the older generations as being the experts, the leaders, the teachers. They are older, wiser, and meet many of the qualifications for "expert." The younger generations are considered "follower" material. In the extended family group, the experts may be any age! Sometimes the expert in the family may be good at only one thing, but that is enough to make him or her qualified. For instance, if a person wants to learn to play and is looking for a qualified leader, who better fits the role than the child. Here is what occurred one night in a Second Family session.

The family members were beginning to filter into the Fellowship Hall from the worship service in the sanctuary. Some of the children had raced in with their usual eagerness and were involving themselves in free play while waiting on the slower members to arrive. Three boys, four and five years of age, were on the stage, which was located at the far end of the room. They had become noisy with their play and occasionally one of their parents would look up to see that no damage was being done. The boys were having a good time running across the stage—just before reaching the wall they would fall to their knees and slide as far as possible. Really good on the knees of the jeans!

As the family members continued to come in, it was obvious that something was really stirring up near the stage area. There was a great deal of noise—laughter, giggling, jumping. This time, several parents looked up and prepared to stop the play. But, the boys were not alone now. They had been joined by one of the grandfathers in the extended family. He was the source of distraction. He was the one causing the laughter and giggles. He had devised a game in which the boys laid on their backs and one by one he would grab their feet and slide them around the stage. Fun, fun, fun! How could the parents interfere. Later, the older man confessed that he had gotten too busy and too serious as an adult and he really wanted to learn to play again. He had gone to the experts in the family—the children.

Children are recognized as leaders in the extended family group and they do respond to the invitation to do their part when the opportunities are made available to them. The children in the Second Family at the Immanuel Baptist Church in Nashville, Tennessee, initiated the request to take on the leadership role for one night's program after they had observed the teenagers planning and leading a session. The coordinators for the extended family group worked with the eight children, who ranged in age from three and a half years to ten years, in scheduling a night. Showing through their outward eagerness to be leaders was the panic of what to do with thirty-five people for an hour and fifteen minutes. That concern and panic is not unique to children.

Since many of the adults had volunteered to design sessions around topics in which they felt some expertise, the coordinators suggested to the children that they choose a topic centered around what they did best. The children replied that their best "thing" was playing. *Play!* The topic was perfect. Not only did the idea pertain to what families do together, but it fit into the larger context of leisure and recreation.

The eight children decided to bring materials and games from home. Two children would be responsible for the activities at a table, with four small groups at work (rather at play). The children said they could provide the refreshments with a little help from mother and dad. One mother and father said they low-keyed their own input into the ideas and plans for the evening, but helped get the materials ready when asked. Another mother and dad replied that they also waited until the children asked them for assistance before entering in the planning—that request came the afternoon prior to the meeting time. Their children had decided on what games and activities they wanted to do but they were unsure about the instruction-giving process. The parents let the children "walk through" the activities and pretended to be followers. That little bit of help seemed to be sufficient.

"The Night the Children Led" was a highlight of the series of programs. The adults and youth made a genuine effort to cooperate without condescending to the younger family members. The learning that occurred for the family members came when they stepped back from the activities and looked at the total effect of the evening. Because some workers with children have asked about the reasons and significance of giving the young children this much responsibility for an evening's program, several concerns are shared about children as teachers and leaders.

Can adults learn from children? In Matthew 11, Jesus is speaking to the crowd gathered around him. He speaks to them of John the Baptist. In his discourse, he asks, "What shall I say about this nation?" He answers the rhetorical question, with an illustration: "These people are like children playing, who say to their little friends, 'We played wedding and you weren't happy, so we played funeral but you weren't sad'" (vv. 16-17).

Jesus finished his statements with a prayer: "O Father, Lord of heaven and earth, thank you for hiding the truth from those who think themselves so wise, and for revealing it to little children. Yes, Father, for it pleased you to do it this way! . . ." (vv. 25-26).

In historical perspective, we may surmise that Jesus learned to keep his inner child in operation. In his teaching he was observant of the children around him. He taught using parables about coins, sheep, seeds and weeds, lilies and birds. He taught us to love the Father, to love one another, to free one another. Where did he learn to see as a child? He learned it from being a child himself. He learned it by growing up in a home with brothers, sisters, mother, and father. He learned it from being with others. He was able to make meaning out of the common events of life.

The children of this world are teachers. In children we

see two qualities. First we see the naturalness—the qualities that persons of all ages want to maintain—spontaneity, faith, trust, belief, awe, wonder, unpretentiousness, the ability to live in the "now." Secondly, we observe in children qualities that they have learned or adapted in order to live in their family, society, and world. Keeping the natural child in operation is difficult because the process of socialization (learning to live in one's world) places many demands upon each person to act in ways other than what may be felt. For the adult to get back some of the naturalness that has been lost, it is sometimes necessary to find a teacher or a guide.

In the extended family, the adults are invited to practice the behaviors of childlikeness. Beware, there is a difference between being "childlike" and being "childish." The adults who have forgotten how to play are invited to join in the game. The adults who have forgotten how to look for the wonders of nature and the simple things of life are invited to look through the eyes of the child. The basic belief that learning can happen from being with others leads to the assumption that adults can learn, or relearn, the qualities of childlikeness from being with and interacting with children. Adults can learn from children.

Is it possible to put too much responsibility on small children? Parents who believe that children learn by doing value their children having opportunities to be planners and leaders. These parents stand ready to help their children reflect and interpret the successes and failures. The children are allowed to go as far as they can in planning with adults providing support from the sidelines. The remarkable and amazing discovery about the children leading out is that they do far more than most adults give them credit for being able to do.

Do children and youth present ideas that are valuable? Have you been a part of a committee where youth were added to give a balance but they were not asked to share their suggestions? Sometimes youth and children get the feeling "they really don't care what I say." In the planning for extended family activities, the opinions and ideas of the younger generation are considered of value because their suggestions keep the sessions from becoming too adult-oriented. Their desire to help and their creativeness are two good reasons for including a youth and a child on every planning team for every session.

In the shared leadership concept all extended family members are given the opportunity to lead out in areas where they feel interest and expertise. The distribution of the planning and leading asks for investment and involvement from everyone, not just a few. The mutual feelings of sometimes I am a leader and sometimes I am a follower are common grounds for relating.

Remember this! In the beginning sessions of the extended family group, state the contract of shared leadership, negotiate the contract where it is necessary, and secure commitments from the children, youth, and adults.

Participators—Not Spectators: Active Participation Concept

"I enjoyed doing things as a group and not sitting in a regular meeting-type setting."

An extended family group is a different way of learning in the church from the regular meeting-type group. At times, the word *unique* is descriptive of this learning setting. The family group looks different from age-graded classes; it looks different from sex-graded classes; and it looks different from classes or groups that just sit in rows. It is not unusual to notice people peeking in the door of the room where the extended family is meeting—especially when the family is having fun, making lots of noise, and exhibiting the aura of excitement. One doorway observer was overheard saying, "I wish I had chosen to join that group this time." Her friend at the doorway responded, "Well, I'm not sure I would like to do all those activities." These observers were weighing decisions and making value judgments as to how participation in the extended family could benefit their lives.

Unfortunately there are a large number of church people (maybe the majority) who have made unconscious decisions not to participate in anything other than Sunday morning activities. These church members will never "peek" their heads in the door to watch the extended family. It does not matter what the purpose of the group is, what the subject is, what the activity is—they block it immediately. These same people who are the most difficult to involve are often the owners of the lonely faces in the congregation. They are the isolated Sunday morning Christians—the age-segregated children and adults, the alienated teenagers. It is very possible that the "Sunday morning syndrome" is the biggest hindrance to the church experiencing "family."

What does participation involve for those persons who do wish to do more than observe from the doorway? What kind of commitment is a person expected to make about attending and participating in the extended family?

Active participation means more than committing oneself to regular attendance in the weekly sessions. In addition to being present, it means committing oneself to being a "doer" when it is our turn to be the follower.

Have you ever had that someone-is-looking-over-my-shoulder feeling? Have you ever said, "Quit staring at me"? Sure, everyone knows about those feelings. Those feelings come when someone is observing us or looking at us. Sometimes we like that feeling. Sometimes we don't! In the extended family activities, everyone is asked to take an active role. Members are asked to join in without being coerced or begged or *made* to participate. Extended family groups are different from groups where a few persons do all the performing and the majority are the spectators.

The spectator element can be a hindrance to some learning. When people are asked to try out a task that is new and difficult, they do not always appreciate an audience. In the extended family, members are often trying on new behaviors or engaging in activities they have not done before (or for a long time). To keep the spectator element from becoming a negative factor, family members are asked to "do" rather than "sit and watch." Leaders or facilitators at each session are encouraged to help members to help each other—participating together. There are times in every group when someone must "sit this one out," but those exceptions are different than having people around who are refusing to become actively involved. Being in extended family is committing oneself to being actively involved.

Active participation means being a "doer" when fulfilling a leadership role. The leader becomes the model for the others. A good motto is: "Don't ask others to do what you, as the leader, are not willing to do yourself." Much of our learning is based upon seeing others, particularly significant others, modeling activities or behaviors. Children are very adept at pointing out to their parents when something is preached but not practiced.

Demonstrating the activity as a part of the instruction-giving process. The leader sometimes can model an activity more quickly than give verbal instructions. The leader indicates his or her willingness to become involved by doing the activity first. Family members see, family members do—"If he can do it, so can I!"

Maintain involvement through use of eye contact and physical presence. The leader can indicate involvement with the language of the body. The eyes can be watchful, the face can indicate approval, the body can give evidence of presence. An obvious illustration of lack of involvement is for the leader to assign the tasks to the group and then sit down to read a book or leave the room.

Join a group after the instructions are given. The interaction among the family members is usually the high point of any activity and leaders *want* to get into the action. The best way for the leader to benefit from the activity is to join in and be a participant. A vivid memory from a Second Family experience describes how a leader can be involved even if participation is limited.

As the members of the extended family group entered the Fellowship Hall, it was obvious that a fun, fun night could be expected. Balloons and streamers criss-crossed the room, areas were arranged with colored paper, baskets, signs, and the knick-knacks of a circus. And, indeed, that was the theme: "Family Night at the Circus." It appeared that the time would be filled with physical activities for the young and old and the in-between. Would everyone participate? Could everyone participate? Looking around at the members of the family one might say that at least two people would have to be spectators. One woman in the group had no arms and another woman, one of the leaders for the circus night, was in a wheelchair. How would these women stomp the balloons and pitch the stuffed animals into the yellow laundry basket? They managed. They asked their family to help them. The lady in the wheelchair held the laundry basket rather than stomp. The lady with no arms let the children throw the ball and she did the running! No child or adult in the room wondered or questioned the involvement of their leader or fellow family member. These ladies knew the secret of being active participants. They were committed to the concept.

Remember this! In the early sessions of forming the extended family group, talk about participation and expectations for involvement, negotiate how much the members can and will give to the concept, and then call forth their commitment.

4
Learning Is Being:
Anyone, Anytime, Anyplace, Anyway

Genius is the ability to see with the eyes of the child and to reason and write about what one sees with the mind and mastery of the adult.

The opposite of genius is the bureaucrat, who sees with the eyes of the adult, reasons with the mind of the child, and writes with the style of the dead.

Thomas Szasz

We are experimenting with an exciting new concept in family life education. It is a new field in education in which people of all ages are involved in learning experiences together. In this family life education we truly try to live out in a creative way the biblical truth that we are a household of faith and the family of God. We know that what happens in the life of one family member has impact on all. Thus, family education cannot be adult education for the adults; it cannot be child education for the children; it ultimately must deal with all the members of the family unit as a total human process in itself.

These statements concerning family life education are part of a letter which was sent to the staff of the Packard Road Baptist Church, Ann Arbor, Michigan, in July of 1977. The church fellowship had expressed an interest in intergenerational groups and a weekend retreat was being set up in August to lead some of the church's families in experientially-based learning activities. More and more often church staff and lay leaders like those at Packard Road Baptist Church are speaking of their concern that emphasis be put on families learning together.

The phrase "experimenting with an exciting new concept in family life education" should not be taken to mean that anything new and different has been discovered. There is nothing new about Christian families gathering to learn about life and faith. What is new is that churches are wanting to put emphasis on helping the members learn in the context of all ages combined rather than all ages separated.

In the excitement of presenting an educational model for learning with people of all ages, there is one important question that must be considered. What is most essential—the learning process or the people who participate? The answer must always be—the people. *Who we are is more important than what we know.*

In the extended family, men, women, boys and girls come together because they are seekers and finders. They are called to be family because of their belief in Jesus Christ. They have the common experience of sharing their faith; and, like the early Christians, they gather to tell of that which they have seen and heard.

That which was from the beginning, which we have heard, which we have seen with our eyes, which we have looked upon and touched with our hands, concerning the word of life—the life was made manifest, and we saw it, and testify to it, and proclaim to you the eternal life which was with the Father and was made manifest to us—that which we have seen and heard we proclaim also to you, so that you may have fellowship with us; and our fellowship is with the Father and with his Son Jesus Christ (1 John 1:1-3, RSV).

In an extended family group, people are always the most important factor. Who they are makes them different and unique. They come from different generations of life—they have been exposed to different life-styles. They are of different ages—some young, some old, some in-between. They are of different maturity levels—physically, mentally, socially, spiritually. We observe their unique differences as they gather in one room and ask, "Why do we think we can design an educational model that can meet the needs of all these people. Where will we begin? What tools do we need?"

Can you imagine what teaching in the early church was like? Very few had religious writings available to them. Not everyone could read. There were no buildings, no sanctuaries, no family activity buildings. There were no teaching helps, no quarterlies with procedures for guiding each session. There was no electricity, no plug-ins or outlets for visual aids. There was no understanding of programs or organizations or small groups. No helpful books about how to be an extended family in the church were available. The teaching was nonstructured, nongraded, and nongrouped. It was unrealistic, impractical, and idealistic. And yet what profound teaching was done!

How do you suppose these early Christian households did so well? How can it be explained? Only one way—through gift. The proclaiming, the writing, the sharing of the faith was dynamic and powerful because it took place under the lordship of Jesus and in the power of the Holy Spirit.

In the extended family, we must never forget the gifts that are given to us—to teach, to study, to proclaim, to have faith, to nurture and heal, to understand, to minister. This family-life education model builds upon belief that "Our bodies have many parts, but the many parts make up only one body when they are all put together" (1 Cor. 12:12, TLB).

With all our studies and research, with all our big terms

for educational techniques and processes, with all our new methods and curriculum guides, we take the chance of forgetting the most essential element. We may forget that the people themselves are the vehicles for passing on the teachings from one age to another. We do not want to forget that people learn from being with other people.

Based upon our belief that people of all ages can learn from each other and build themselves up through their common experiences, we present the following assumptions about learning in the extended family.

Learning Is Being

What is learning? What do you believe about learning? A belief about learning that characterizes our approach to extended family experiences is that learning is happening at any time, in any place, and to anyone—learning is being.

People—human beings—are always learning. This learning is affecting our values, our attitudes, our behaviors, and our beliefs. This learning produces change. This *learning produces growth.*

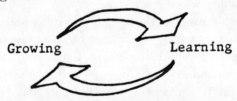

Growing   Learning

Likewise, the human growth process (maturation, development) creates desires, motivations, and attitudes for gaining new learning. When this part of the cycle occurs, *growth produces learning.*

The belief that learning is being and that learning produces changes in a person leads to the assumption that one individual has the potential to influence another human being. This belief, when put in the context of a nuclear or extended family relationship, would account for a statement such as: "What happens in the life of one family member has impact on all." It matters not whether we are placed in a certain family by birth or whether we choose a certain family group. In the midst of these familial relationships, we can learn; we can change; we can influence.

Learning Is a Flowing Together

After the people of God left Egypt, the adults were told to teach God's commandments to those who would come after them. In Deuteronomy 11:18-21, we find an early religious education model:

So keep these commandments carefully in mind. Tie them to your hand to remind you to obey them, and tie them to your forehead between your eyes! Teach them to your children. Talk about them when you are sitting at home, when you are out walking, at bedtime, and before breakfast! Write them upon the doors of your houses and upon your gates, so that as long as there is sky above the earth, you and your children will enjoy the good life awaiting you in the land the Lord has promised you.

Long before our modern education theorists began telling us how to teach, the writer of the Old Testament story shares a method for instructing our children in the faith. We are to have reminders available to us at all times. The commandments are to be visible. We are to talk about them to our children—not just in the classroom on Sunday, but also when we are sitting at home. As we walk together in the woods and along city streets, as we tuck our children into bed at night, as we serve the instant oatmeal and eggs for breakfast, we are to talk of God. We are to write the commandments so we can use them at home and have them as we go through the gates out into the world.

Our efforts at educating our offspring will be rewarded.

The promise to the Hebrew parents in the wilderness was that a good life would be awaiting for them and their children in the land that God had promised. For the parents of the contemporary family of God, the promise of the New Testament is that parents and children who believe in Jesus will share eternal life.

The Old Testament processes for instructing others about matters of the faith would fit well into the contemporary process called confluent education.

con-flu-ence n. 1. a coming or flowing together; meeting, or gathering at one point. 2. the flowing together of two or more streams, the meeting place of two streams, the combined stream formed by conjunction.

In technical language, confluent education is the flowing together of cognitive and affective learning. In the language of the Old Testament, it is the head knowledge and the heart knowledge. Like two fast-flowing streams coming together out of the hills and joining into one quiet river in the valley, the knowledge of the head and the knowledge from the heart flow together to become the learning necessary for the living of one's life. The emotion flows together with the intellect.

The learning is fluid like a river is fluid. The learning is in solution and mingles and mixes. What one learns in childhood mixes with what one learns in youth. The combination of learning from childhood and youth blends into the knowing that comes with the experiences in adulthood. The learning is being.

There is a wholeness in knowing facts and feelings. Loss is felt when one of the areas becomes stagnant and static. The person who has lost the ability to feel is a person to be pitied. The person who cannot learn with the mind is one who needs aid.

In the extended family, the time together is spent sharing our inner feelings of the heart with other people. We talk and tell what we feel. We listen and try to understand what another is feeling inside. It is an "inner-state system." I share my "inner state" and you listen. You share your "inner state" and I listen. From this sharing we learn.

We learn more from each other by sharing feelings than from sharing facts and information from our minds. We often learn useable facts as a by-product. We learn a recipe for making bread but we learned it because we are attempting to share feelings about how bread affects us—daily bread, the bread of heaven, manna in the wilderness. We learn how to make a cross out of two small trees (fact and skill) but we are attempting to learn how we feel and how others feel about the place of the cross in our lives. Our learning is never separated from our mind and heart. They are allowed to flow and mingle.

A basic assumption about education in the extended family model is that learning comes from a flowing together of what we know with our minds and what we feel with the heart.

Learning Is Based on Sameness

When the first Christian families joined together because of their common experience of faith, they broke bread, had fellowship one with another, sang hymns, and told their stories. They found the common threads of life and built upon these when they came together. What does the extended family group have in common and how are these common grounds used in the educational process?

People share in their basic needs for existence—food and water, air to breathe, time for rest, shelter from the heat and cold, security and love, the need to be needed, and a purpose for living. Some of these needs the extended family can fulfill, while other needs must be met outside the group. Whether our goal is to meet the basic needs of the extended family members or not, these needs are utilized as topics for learning together. If a list of study topics is developed in the extended family planning session, many of these study suggestions will deal with basic needs common to all ages.

What else do people of all ages have in common? They have feelings. Young and old alike share a common ground in their feelings. In *Peoplemaking,* Virginia Satir says: "Every human being feels. It may not always show, but it's there. And the faith that it is there even though you can't see it can make you act differently from the way you would have if you reacted only to what shows." [1]

In the extended family group, we can relate to one another because of our mutual feelings. We all feel pain. We all feel joy. We all feel sad. We all feel frustrated and anxious. We all feel sleepy. We all feel hunger. We feel. We can plan our learning experiences to center around how we feel. We *feel* our way into learning. This is using the feelings from our heart knowledge to learn the facts for our head knowledge. It means using the senses to stimulate our feelings. In the extended family we use our bodies as well as our minds.

At all times, religious educators are made aware of the differences in people when all the ages are brought together. Too often when decisions are made to educate the congregation the groups are formed to make the differences less obvious. All the children go to one room. The boys between nine years and eighteen years are separated from girls of nine through eighteen; men and women are divided by their ages. People are taught easier when they have more in common. That is a well-known and often-followed philosophy of education. It would be just as difficult for a twelve-year old today to be found in a men's Fellowship Class as it was for Mary and Joseph to find Jesus in the Temple with the elders of his religious system. Supposedly the differences between twelve-year-old boys and older men are too great to be handled efficiently in one class.

The extended family group attempts to follow the principle of looking for common ground for its educational objectives. It seeks to find common experiences that all can share regardless of sex or age. Thus, the basic assumption about education in the extended family is that learning is based upon sameness.

Learning Is Informal

If one holds to the theory that learning is being and that learning is taking place all the time, then it would be possible to assume that learning can happen any place and in the presence of anyone (or no one). If we could separate our learning between formal and informal learning settings and then make a graph, we would see that the larger portion of our learning is informal and unplanned. We learn from our world and the people in the world. We learn from being and interacting with other people.

In our many trips back to New Orleans, we stay with the Lee family. Ann Lee, who died of cancer in 1973, was a remarkable teacher of outside-the-classroom information. The last Christmas before her death, she was preparing for the annual extended family Christmas dinner—which always included twenty or more people. Since there was a morning worship at the church on Christmas Day, she prepared the dining room tables the evening before. This particular Christmas, Ann was functioning without her sight—blindness brought about by cancer. In the late afternoon of Christmas Eve she called Melissa, who was six years old, and Jud, who was almost four years old, to come in the dining room to help her set the tables. She entrusted their small fingers with her finest crystal and china. As she handed out plates, goblets, and cups from the china cabinet, the helpers carried them to the tables and put them in place. With loving guidance, she instructed them where to lay each piece of silver.

When the table was set, she asked, "How does it look?" Taking great joy in their handiwork, Melissa and Jud described a scene that Ann had designed in her mind. Ann may have lost some of her ability to maneuver the dishes into place, but she had not lost her remarkable ability to teach the next generation the art of preparing for a feast. The children were learning from a loving person how to set a table. They were learning the joy of working together on a celebration in the warm context of the family.

Over and over again, we find ourselves learning something that we did not set out to learn. We observe children learning unexpectedly. Sometimes we are surprised when people learn things that no one intended for them to learn.

The smaller portion of our learning occurs in the formal setting—the classroom, the lecture halls, laboratories and other places designated for learning. Both the formal and informal settings are desirable learning environments. The extended family has some of the characteristics of a planned, intentionally designed, structured group. Because extended family members seem to learn best in the informal atmosphere similar to that of a warm, loving home, the belief about learning is that the setting should be informal. To intentionally plan for a setting to achieve certain objectives it is necessary to have an awareness of what can be done to design these environments.

As you form an extended family experience in the church, consider your own involvement in learning settings. How much are you influenced by your surroundings? Do you act one way in one place and another way in a different setting? Can you recall laughing and joking in the Fellowship Hall only to walk down the corridor to the sanctuary and find yourself quiet and calm? What happened to make the difference? The walk took only a matter of minutes. It was maybe a distance of a few feet. Why did your behavior change? You know the answer already. The environment of one part of the church called for a behavior different than the other environment. The settings and the expectations changed in a matter of minutes and within a few feet, and you had learned to make the change in your actions.

In the extended family, the goal is to create an atmosphere of informality which is conducive to learning from one another. To achieve this objective, it is necessary to plan the setting.

When our children come home from school in the midafternoon, the action around our house picks up. They are eating, talking loudly with their friends, practicing cheers, and jumping around. Their behavior is close to uncontrolled and I wonder occasionally if they have been that way in the classroom. Poor teacher. When we talk about the difference in their home behavior and their school behavior, they assure me that they have been relatively quiet and "proper" for their teachers. They say that coming home makes a difference. They can let loose! The difference between the formal learning and informal learning settings allows them to behave differently. Learning can and does happen in both of those settings. The people, the physical space, the objects or lack of objects in the space, and purpose for being in the setting influence the behavior.

What does our knowledge about the setting and its influence on our behavior mean in designing a place of learning for the extended family group?

First, we must intentionally plan the physical space. If we are striving to build relationships among persons, the space must facilitate this goal. Persons who sit in a sanctuary with pews facing toward the front have a difficult time talking (they do manage, however). Fewer possibilities for face-to-face interactions are allowed when chairs are fixed and are facing one way. We learn, then, to put the extended family in a large space where the furniture is movable and the use of space is flexible. Sometimes the chairs are in circles for a large group, sometimes they are around work tables, sometimes they are in small circles of five to eight, sometimes there are no pieces of furniture in the room. A certain amount of flexibility is available in most rooms of the church, but for the extended family select one that has a lot of flexibility.

A principle of space in the extended family model is that "less is more." That means we look at the *fit* between the physical surrounding and the purpose of the group. The most important learning tools in the extended family are the people themselves. We are purposefully bringing people together to learn from each other, anyway, anytime. Any other learning tools that get in the way of this purpose are called "clutter."

To make the setting fit the purpose of the extended family, get rid of the clutter. If chairs keep people apart, get rid of the chairs. If tables get in the way of knee-to-knee activities and conversation, get rid of the tables. If the fun and game activities keep people from learning from each other, then change the activities. If the food prevents people from having time to purposefully interact, then cut down on the refreshments.

The proper fit in the extended family is to provide an environment where people see people and people interact with people, without distraction from outside sources. In planning the setting, use only those physical learning aids and tools which fit the main purpose.

The second assumption about planning a warm, informal

learning setting deals with the way people "feel" about the setting. Will people come into the room (the physical space) and feel warm and comfortable in the extended family group?

One of the local restaurants in our town features a commercial on television that begins something like this: "From the minute you walk in, you can feel right at home." This is the objective for the extended family group—to make people feel at home. The assumed part of that objective is that people see their homes as being warm, loving, and positive. There are people who do not like their homes in real life. Most of us, however, hold to an idealistic picture of home being comfortable, cozy, and caring. The extended family wants, in reality, to meet the ideal expectation.

How do we achieve this feeling of warmth? Primarily, people are seen and appreciated for who they are. The people, regardless of their age, wealth, knowledge, ability, or physical form, are important. Each one is greeted and treated as a person to be loved. Everyone is an authority—"I may not know anything about you, but I am the best authority on me."

In the extended family, it is all right to be yourself. And, it is all right to try to be different. In some groups, we must act certain ways because we "have to" but in this group it is openly acceptable to try to be something else. The members are encouraged to try new behaviors and new ways of thinking.

In the Second Family groups, members have been encouraged to change their names if they wish. In the Bible, the changing of a person's name was connected to the role that the person fulfilled or a personality trait that was being emphasized. Many interesting stories can be shared about family members who had changes in their names.

Albert McClellan, who has been mentioned earlier in his

role as a co-designer of several Second Family groups, is now known as "Abba" by many of the people in his church and family. In the very first session of the extended family group, he put the word "Abba" on his name tag and explained its meaning as being a familiar or endearing term for father in the Hebrew language. Albert was indeed a father to many in the Second Family and the name fit him well.

The ability to feel warm and comfortable in the extended family might happen by chance because there are factors at work in small groups of people that bring about good feelings. Because in other intergenerational groups it sometimes is just assumed that this warm feeling will be a by-product, the basic belief about learning within the context of the extended family is that the warm and informal setting is preferred and that it can be achieved most often by intentionally planning for it to happen.

Learning Is from Friends and Models

"Jesus loves me, this I know. . . ." How do you know that? ". . . for the Bible tells me so." This little song out of our childhood is a perfect example of learning from an authority that is creditable. Philosophers and educators spend many hours discussing our sources of knowing. One of the ways that we learn is obvious to most of us—we learn from authorities. The Bible is one authority. It is a book that is believed in and trusted to be correct. Parents are authorities. We learn from our parents because we trust and respect them, because we need them and fear them. We learn from teachers and leaders in the school and church because they have authority, training, and respect.

In the extended family, we learn from the authorities in the group. If we want to learn to play, we look to the experts who are most often our children and youth. If we want to learn more about the Bible and God, we look to the scholars and Christian disciples in the group. The authorities may be of any age.

As we learn in the extended family, we are relating to persons in a family-like setting. To facilitate learning, the authorities are asked to teach not as powerful, intellectual, "know-it-all" experts—but as one friend to another friend. The term, friend, best reflects a relationship of mutual listening, expressing, and caring. The friend relationship can exist across the generations as well as between two members of the same generation. The friend relationship can exist between two persons from the same immediate family—a father can use the opportunity to teach his son as a friend. The son can be given the chance to learn not as a child of the father but as a friend of an older man. This style of teaching may need to be consciously learned and practiced by some adults who are accustomed to teaching by the authority placed in them as educators or parents. For the adult to teach the child in the friend relationship it does not require a "coming down" to the child's level; it requires being an adult who can accept, value, and respect the child as a person.

Some of our best and quickest learning comes from people to whom we are closely related or to whom we have deep feelings of affection. In the warm, friendly relationship between children and adults, the teachers can become models for our learning. Parents who are desirous of their children seeing the faith lived out by persons other than themselves can appreciate the extended family group in the church. For with this group, faith is lived as well as shared verbally.

One teaching technique that fits so well into the extended family education model is storytelling. Everyone of every age loves a story. In many of the sessions there should be opportunities for stories to be related. Along with well-known and well-loved stories from the Bible and classical literature, the people in the extended family can be encouraged to share their stories. Time after time in previous Second Family experiences, the storytelling takes on an added dimension that is rarely found in a formal classroom setting. The group dynamic that best can describe what happens in these storytelling sessions is that the verbal telling has been enhanced by the relationships that have been formed along the family members. Rather than just being the teller of fascinating tales, the storyteller becomes a living model for the family members. This "extra" plus in the teaching technique can only be explained by the feeling that flows together with the facts—confluence.

The basic belief about learning that has developed from observing different sources of authoritative teaching is that the teachers are most effective when they become friends and models.

Learning Is Reflecting on Experiences

Earlier in this chapter it was stated that the people in the extended family are called to be family because of their common belief in Jesus as Savior. The passage from 1 John 1:1-3 was given as an example of how this faith has been shared with us. Read the passage again. This time notice the italicized words that indicate how concretely the early Christians described their experience.

That which was from the beginning, which we have *heard*, which we have *seen* with our *eyes*, which we have *looked* upon and *touched* with our *hands*, concerning the *word* of life—the life was made manifest, and we *saw* it, and *testify* to it, and *proclaim* to you the eternal life which was with the Father and was made manifest to us—that which we have *seen* and *heard* we *proclaim* also to you, so that you may have *fellowship* with us; and our *fellowship* is with the Father and with his Son Jesus Christ (RSV).

A large portion of the learning in the extended family group is experiential. Because the moments together are built around concrete activities that the young and old can participate in together, learning comes from doing and reflecting.

In experiential learning there are no specific answers to many of the questions. Unlike some learning in which two-plus-two-equals-four answers are given, in experiential learning many of the answers are subjective. A mother may say to her child, "Oh, that is a beautiful picture. You have done a good job." Yet the child may have tears in her eyes and keep repeating, "I don't make good pictures. That is awful." No amount of coercing will change the child's feelings and there is no right way the child should feel. Questions and reflection might provide learning as to why the child feels one way and the mother feels another way about the picture.

Children in the extended family are often the least "experienced" and they will benefit from the guidance of an adult or youth who can help them verbalize the questions that aid reflection. The phrase "Ours not to question why; ours but to do, or die" is not an appealing concept to those leaders who believe in experiential education. For to question is to surface the feelings, the sensations, the effect that has been brought about by a happening. The questions are the tools to aid the learning process.

In learning from our experiences, we cannot say that everyone is going to learn the same thing. People experience differently. They arrive at different conclusions to answers. They perceive situations from different viewpoints. In the sharing of feelings and insights about an experience, each person must be allowed the opportunity to express what he or she feels or senses. Children must be heard patiently for they often feel or sense something but have difficulty formulating the words to convey their innermost feelings.

In assisting children to express themselves about an experience, it is often helpful to engage them in an activity with which they are familiar—drawing, painting pictures, modeling with clay, acting out scenes. Many times adults find these concrete methods of expressing feelings to be a refreshing change from just "talking" about what has happened.

There are many ways to debrief a concrete experience. To debrief means to think about, reflect upon, and gather insights from an experience. Some techniques for debriefing are not suitable for intergenerational groups because of the limited abilities of some members. Writing a long paragraph about a happening could be an ordeal for a second grader. Reading lines from a script is difficult for younger children. Simulations and related activities that contain abstract words and concepts must also be eliminated. The debriefing methods that work best are those that are quick to do, simple to answer, and deal with concrete instructions and terms.

Experience Questions. Experience questions get at personal opinions, attitudes, actions, feelings, and beliefs. The questions are asked about a situation that has happened. The questions generally use the word *you*.

Lead the extended family in the following experience, and then use experience questions to discover how they feel or react to their experience. This game is called Prui and is found in the *New Games Book* (see Additional Resources). In this game, the family members are trying to find a creature named Prui. The game will allow members of all ages to engage in a contact game.

To begin the game, invite everyone in the extended family to stand in a large circle. Tell them to close their eyes and begin milling around. When they bump into someone, they are to shake his or her hand and ask, "Prui?" If the other person asks "Prui?" back, then you have not found the Prui creature. Keeping the eyes closed, find another person to ask.

With everyone bumping around, shaking hands, and asking "Prui? Prui?"—the leader whispers to one of the family members to become the Prui. The Prui can see, so the Prui walks around with his or her eyes open. The Prui can see, but cannot talk. When someone bumps into the Prui, shakes hands, and asks "Prui?" the Prui remains silent. The player who received no answer, will ask again, "Prui?" No response, a second time. The player has found the Prui and now can open his or her eyes and becomes a Prui, too. The Pruis join together by holding hands. Then when someone bumps into the Prui, they must find their way to the end of the string of Pruis and shake one of the end hands, asking "Prui?" If players bump into two or more silent persons with clasped hands, they know they have the Prui somewhere in the middle. They must feel their way to the end and join it.

Soon, all the family members will happily be holding hands, with the exception of one or two persons who will be wandering off in some far part of the room. When the last member becomes a part of the Prui creature, a big yell signifies the end.

Ask the family members to form small groups and talk about Prui. Here are some questions that could be offered to the members as suggestions:

How did you feel when you were asked to join in a game? Do you like playing games? Had you played the game? What about the game did you like best of all? Were you one of the first or last to find the Prui? How would you feel if you never became a part of the Prui creature? How would you change the game to make it better? Can you teach this game to others now that you have tried it?

Unfinished Sentences. An incomplete sentence offers part of a sentence and invites the extended family members to complete it the way that seems appropriate to them. Keep unfinished sentences as open-ended as possible. There are many ways to involve people in unfinished sentences and almost any topic can stimulate the beginning sentence stems.

Try the following technique for allowing extended family members to speak one-to-one. The topic for these questions will be "Life in My Family."

Ask the family members to number off by twos—one, two, one, two. The "one" group will take their chairs and form a circle. The chairs should have the backs to the center so the family members will be facing outward. Instruct the "two" group to bring their chairs and place them in the outer circle facing the persons in the inner circle. Everyone should be facing a partner. This is a variation of the double circle. Big adults and little children standing in a double circle are not on the same eye level. Sitting in the chairs helps persons to see one another—face-to-face.

Tell the family members that you will give a part of a sentence and they are to complete the sentence. Give them a minute to talk together on the topic. Call time!

Ask the outer circle of persons to get up and move one person to the right. Give another question. Allow them another minute to talk. Repeat the process. Here are some questions which all ages can complete:

1. The most important person in my family is . . .
2. On Saturday morning, my family . . .
3. This summer, I wish my family would . . .
4. One television show that all my family watches . . .
5. Our toothbrushes are . . .
6. A food that everyone in our family eats is . . .
7. If I am alone at home, I . . .
8. The place in my house that I like best . . .
9. Making up the bed is . . .
10. The thing I like best about my family is . . .

Cartoons. Cartoons with blank dialogue are always fun, exciting ways of talking about an experience. Children who enjoy drawing can find this an easy way to express themselves. For the nonartist family member, empty balloons can be drawn on a paper and filled in with dialogue. The object is to get out feelings about what happened and not to win an art contest.

Lists. Lists invite the family members to brainstorm or think of a number of items in a category. The lists can be used to find out how members feel about general categories (events that have happened to everyone) or lists can be used to find out how persons feel about a specific situation (an event that has just happened in the group).

Make a copy of the following story for each of the small family groups:

"The Happy Pencil"

There was a happy pencil that lived in a little blue case with all the nice little friends that he knew. One day a boy named Joe bought him. Joe took him to the classroom and sharpened him up.

The teacher said, "Joe, you will need to turn this homework in tomorrow." Joe went home on the school bus. He went to sleep that night and his homework was not done. The pencil got up, flew over to the paper, and wrote what Joe needed to write.

When Joe went to school the next morning, he said, "Miss Fern, I don't have my homework done." She looked at his paper and said, "You *do* have it done."

Then the little pencil smiled.

—Jud Hendrix
Third Grader

Ask one person in each of the groups to read the story. Ask one person in each group to be prepared to record responses on a newsprint. The story tells about a "helping pencil." Ask the members to listen to the story and think of all the things they have done this past week which were "helping actions." Ask them to prepare a group list. After the list is completed, ask the family members to look over the list and as a group to decide on several helping actions that make them feel particularly happy. Draw a "happy face" beside these actions.

The belief that learning comes from the reflections upon concrete experiences necessitates planning for action to take place within the extended family's time together. The members become doers. We do not just talk about dirt and water. We get our hands dirty by planting seeds in soil and then we talk about our feelings. We do not just tell about how much fun we have at parties, we have a party and then share our feelings. The concrete experiences of the extended family as it meets together in a weekly session and the happenings that occur in the everyday world of the members become the building blocks for learning when persons of all ages reflect together.

Learning Is Planned

It just will not work if you do not plan! The simple truth about extended family learning and programming is that it takes hard work and good planning.

The extended family model is similar to an open-class education model in that deliberate, purposeful planning is needed to achieve certain goals and objectives. What often appears to be an unstructured group is actually very structured. It takes careful planning for a group to look and to feel free and flexible.

Finding the correct tension between too much structuring and too little structuring is important to the success of the extended family. One family member evaluated her experience by saying, "Activities and plans needed more structure so all participants would know what was expected of them." Another evaluation said: "Programming can be free, easy, unencumbered, and innovative. The looseness and flexibility of the organization was a strength."

A suggestion for blending the structured and unstructured characteristics is to build a good plan sheet, framework, or general format. Some of this planning can be done initially by the coordinators of the event. Other parts of the planning can be done in the first sessions as the weekly session topics are outlined. Additional planning is done by the weekly leadership teams made up of people of all ages. Planning is continuously being done as feedback and evaluations are given from week to week or at periodical "check" points in the experience together.

Although thorough planning at each point along the way is essential, each part of the plan must be subject to change— if a change becomes necessary. A flexible plan defines what kind of activity will be used at a specific time, what supplies will be needed, and what the purpose is for each activity;

but the plan allows for the participants to decide the final outcome. The plan brings the people together, but it allows the spirit to invade and fill the form.

Individuals who think that planned events cannot allow room for the unplanned to happen have not been in a Second Family group. Time after time the unexpected occurs. Time after time, the old familiar songs, activities, games, and stories take on a newness. Let me share a memory:

The extended family had gathered in the Fellowship Hall. The study for the evening was based on the events preceding Jesus' death on the cross. The family groups had worked on activities around the tables. One group made a reconstruction of the Temple in Jerusalem using maps, Bible information, cardboard, clay, pieces of wood, and much imagination. Another group had constructed a cross from pieces of a tree. A third group studied the symbols of the cross, and the fourth group had looked at songs, poems, and literature of the cross.

Upon completion of their projects, the small groups joined together for the sharing and reporting time. The family groups had gone far beyond expectations in working on the assignments which had been suggested for them. It was obvious that the leaders for that evening had not been aware of just how much creativity and motivation the family members were capable of exerting. The excitement and appreciation of what each member had done was becoming quite obvious—it could be felt!

The plan for the session was that the story of the disciples and Jesus at the Last Supper in the upper room would be told by the oldest member of the extended family. She was a retired seminary professor, who spoke in a slow, precise manner. She was gray-haired, tall, erect, and stately in appearance. A gracious lady. She had prepared for her story.

She had even spent time apart from the group activities that night to make sure she knew what she wanted to say. She had planned.

When the time came for the story, she asked that a folding chair be placed in the middle of the semicircle of chairs and she motioned all the family members to draw toward her. The adults scooted their chairs closer. The children and youth sat right at her feet. The picture of the family is just what you would see in a dream. It was perfect. And then, out of the plan, out of the structure, came the unplanned—the filling of the form by the Spirit of the Living God. For as the story began and the wise teacher began to share her insights about Jesus as the elder brother of the disciples, the extended family took on the aura of the family of God gathered together.

The youngest child sat immovable with eyes and ears attuned to the storyteller. The dismissal bell rang in the room but the noise did not interrupt. The movement of persons leaving other rooms could be heard in the hallway. Still the family lingered on and listened. And in the telling of the story came the experience of knowing that God was filling the midst. For many family members, that night will live on as a time when Jesus' presence, as the elder brother in the family of God, became a reality. The planning had been done. The process had been thought out. The unexpected had happened. And it can happen again, and again, and again.

5
The Church As Family:
Getting Started

I was told by the man that stands at the gate at the head of this way, that, if I called here, you would show me excellent things, such as would help me on my journey.

John Bunyan

___ 1. Make a List

I have a friend who makes a list when she has a lot to do in a short period of time. Perhaps you organize yourself in that way too. When my friend makes her lists, she always has the same first entry.

___ 1. Make a list

After she adds the other items, she goes back and checks off the first entry. She has started. She is on her way to accomplishing what she sets out to do. There is a lesson to be learned from my friend.

Checklist

___ 1. Make a list.
___ 2. Assess need for extended family and find out who is interested. (Make another list.)
___ 3. Secure leadership. (Train, if necessary.)
___ 4. Decide on theme, time, and place. (Framework, only.)
___ 5. Publicize the event.
___ 6. Seek commitments through letters and telephone calls.
___ 7. Finalize the plans.

This chapter is a checklist for starting an extended family group. Check the tasks off—one by one. You will be on your way to "getting started."

_____ 2. Assess Needs and Interest

If the need for an extended family is surfacing from the members of the church congregation, there are usually several families who are saying, "We would like to try an extended family group because . . . ." These four or five individuals can become the catalysts, the coordinators, or the leadership team that gets the intergenerational group started. The church staff leaders should be involved in the initial planning of the group. Administrative decisions about space, scheduling of another group into the church program, budget allocations, and related matters can be worked out in the beginning.

In some churches, the extended family will be initiated by the church staff leaders. The intergenerational approach might be the answer to needs that are present in the educational ministry. Low attendance, new-member orientation, family-life education emphases, and strengthening of relationships among the families of the church are just a few reasons to use the extended family group as an optional approach to education and outreach. The staff leaders who wish to try an extended family experience will want to enlist the assistance of laypersons who are open to trying educational methods that are different from many they are accustomed to using. Sometimes there are persons in the congregation who have requested small group involvement of any kind. These persons already own an idea or vision that can be channelled through the extended family model and they are generally more ready to buy in to something new. They are willing to invest themselves in the small group concept. This investment is important in making any new idea become a reality.

Make another list. On this list, write down all the family units of the church. List each person within the immediate families. Fit each person into an age category: preschool (1-5 years), children (6-12), youth (13-17), young adult (18-29), median adult (30-50), older adult (50 and over). The age groups vary within each church family and within organizations. They are given here as suggestions only.

From the list of persons and ages, determine which families might be the most interested in an extended family group. This list will be of great value when the contacts are made for obtaining a core group of persons who will commit themselves to the extended family idea. Conscious effort is made to first contact families and individuals who say they are *very interested* in the family group. Most often, these are the "seekers" who are willing to step out to make something happen in their lives.

____ 3. Secure Leadership

Sharing leadership is basic to the extended family model! Even though all members of the group will be asked to share in the responsibilities for leading the group, somebody or several "somebodies" will need to share the leadership of the group and wear a title of some kind.

Titles for leaders of the extended family are many: codirectors, coordinators, coleaders, leadership team, or "head honchos." The number of persons who share the major leadership role varies. The following suggested combinations have been tried by extended family groups. Regardless of who leads, one criteria for leaders is that they also be participants in the group and give the same commitment that is expected of others.

- church staff leader (minister of education, pastor, youth director)
- two-couple team (husband and wife team from two families)

• two-family team (all members of two families)
• coordinating team (two to six individuals)

Although every extended family will utilize their leadership in different ways, there are several tasks that need to be handled. These tasks include:

Housekeeping Chores. Just like with the family at home, some important matters must be cared for regularly—making announcements, changing plans and schedules, sending out letters and information to absentee family members, making sure the meeting place is cleaned up and ready for the next users, turning off the lights and closing the doors when the meeting is over.

Liaison Responsibilities. The leadership of the extended family will cooperate with the church council or church staff in clearing schedules, presenting material for use in record-keeping, turning in announcements of events, securing supplies and resources through proper channels, working within a designated budget, and other administrative matters.

Responsibilities for Programming. The framework for the extended family group needs to be constructed. The leaders then work behind the scenes, in any way necessary, to help members of the family assume the shared responsibility of filling in the framework—leadership teams must be organized for planning weekly programs and special events. In the beginning sessions, the leaders must be highly visible as they model techniques and methods which are essential to this particular approach to teaching and learning.

Qualities of a Good Leader

What are good qualities for a leader of the extended family experience to possess? Can just anybody lead this diverse group of individuals? Will just anyone *want* to lead a group with all ages represented?

An extended family group in the church is a somewhat

unique group of people. Not everybody will want to work with this group and not everybody is qualified to work with them. There are certain qualities that make persons good leaders of an intergenerational group. Granted, not every person will be gifted or capable in all of the six areas mentioned below, but when several persons in leadership roles possess one or two of these characteristics, the team will be strong and effective.

Sensing the need for an extended family.— The individuals who want to be in an extended family because of what the group can do for them personally will often be more willing to invest the time and effort that is necessary to make the group work. The need is a force which drives, impels, and compels persons to do things they never dreamed they could do. A good leader for the extended family is one who has a dream, a hope, an idea, a need.

Creativity and/or adaptibility.—Much of the designing of an extended family group comes from adapting resources (program ideas, curriculum materials, books, films) which are available for leading age groups in church, school, or community organizations. What cannot be adapted for the extended family's use, must be created new. Although this quality sounds like a "rare" quality, most of us do this in our work and family living anyway. We are just too modest to say we are "good" at doing creative thinking and planning.

Knowledge of group process.—The extended family group is a small group. It is a group in which persons encounter one another at levels that range from being newly acquainted to being deeply involved. Some people know each other just a little bit—maybe by sight. Some members, particularly those who have persons from their immediate family in the group, will have deep attachments and emotional feelings for certain people. Knowledge of what can and does happen in small groups is helpful. Printed resources for small group work are available. Persons who wish to gain more skills in group process might consider attending training sessions in the local church or going to a training seminar/ workshop. Many small group seminars are held by churches, schools, or business organizations.

Knowledge of developmental tasks for each age group.— What makes the five-year-old different from the sixty-five-year-old in the area of motor coordination. How much abstract thinking can the twelve-year-old do? Most parents have some experiential knowledge about growth patterns. Some adults in the extended family will have the training and educational background for working with the age groups. Knowledge of developmental stages is valuable in planning the activities for persons who are in all stages of maturation.

Skill in seeking out and securing resources.—Program ideas, films, books—supplies like paper and scissors—all these resources make the extended family a fun, exciting, active learning group. Having persons on the leadership team who can gather information and supplies makes the task much simpler.

Skill in keeping a general group framework intact while allowing for shared leadership.—One church learned from their first extended family experience, that someone must be able to see the "whole" while allowing the "parts" to function. To make this extended family experience a strong positive experience a leader must know how to coordinate the parts. If the structure is too loose or too tight, the effectiveness is lessened. The ability to let things happen with the planning and with the activities while still maintaining a direction is an essential quality for leaders.

Securing Training for Extended Family Leaders

Being in an extended family group is the best training. It is experiential training. Doing it and learning from the successes and failures. Experiential training can be received by:

(1) participating in a group
(2) attending a workshop held at denominational training centers or attending area workshops led by trained leaders
(3) inviting trained leaders to conduct a weekend retreat or local church workshop

____ 4. Decide on Theme, Time, and Place

A framework for the extended family group can be a very loose, open structure. The framework is essential to getting the group started and it is essential to keeping the group together. One leader of an extended family experience said:

"Coordination of the total event was lacking in our first attempt at doing an extended family group. Because no persons or teams were in charge of guiding the programming and connecting the weekly sessions together, we struggled to maintain our course."

Basic items to include in the framework are:

1. *Name for the group* (examples: Second Family, Extended Family, Summer Family, Fun Family)
2. *Theme or focus* (examples: "Celebrating the Holidays," "Fun Family Worship," "Seven Sundays of Summer," "Thank You, God . . .")
3. *Duration of group* (examples: four weeks, six weeks, three months)
4. *Meeting place and time* (examples: Sundays, 6:00-7:30 P.M., Fellowship Hall of _____ Church.

Choosing a Theme or Focus

"In extended family we do together what families do!" That statement is a good rule-of-thumb for designing events for the extended family. Gear the activities, the Bible study, the topics of interest—everything—toward doing what families do when they are together. Families do a multitude of things and the choices are numerous.

The selection of a theme provides: (1) information which helps participants decide when, how, where, or if they can "plug in" during the experience; (2) a basic structure that can be filled in later by the family members as they assume their roles as leaders and experts; and (3) continuity, allowing the parts to become meaningfully related to the whole and allowing the weekly sessions to build upon the main topic.

Four general categories for theme selections are offered for your use in planning frameworks. In each category, skeleton outlines are given with a unit title and four or five session titles.

Holiday emphasis.—Holidays and family traditions are important to family life. The Christmas season and Easter observance are two special events in the Christian community of believers and in the households of immediate families. Resource materials for intergenerational groups are usually available in these two theme areas.

Light of the World
1. Light of Hope of the Prophets
2. Light and Warmth from the Stable
3. Light That Surrounded the Shepherds
4. Light that Guided the Wise Men

I Walked Today Where Jesus Walked
1. Bethlehem (birth)
2. Nazareth (childhood and youth)
3. Caesarea Philippi (ministry)
4. Jerusalem (cross and (resurrection, Easter)

Harvest Time
1. Apples and Johnny Appleseed—(an all-apple meal)
2. Scarecrows (what to be afraid of)
3. Thanksgiving

Celebrate the Summer
1. The Sights of Summer
2. The Feel of Summer
3. The Sounds of Summer
4. The Tastes and Smells of Summer

4. When the Saints Go March-
   ing In—(family trees,
   ancestors)

Topics-of-interest.—To discover common areas of interest for the extended family, brainstorm the question "What do families do?" They play ball, go fishing, eat together, camp, build things, share hobbies—on and on the list goes. In planning with the extended family, put up a large sheet of newsprint and let members call out things that interest and concern them. Or, divide up into small groups and make posters from magazine pictures and word art telling of each one's interests. Look at the posters and write down some of the common areas. Ask persons to volunteer their "expertise" in planning and leading a session on a topic they enjoy.

Every Person an Artist
1. Music
2. Paper Construction
3. Photography, Slides,
   Films
4. Puppets and/or Drama
5. Arts Festival (alternate)

The Great Outdoors
1. Camping and Hiking
2. In Our Backyard
   (lawns and patios)
3. Outdoor Drama or Music
4. The Great Fisherman
   (Simon Peter and other
   disciples)

Field Trips
1. Parks
2. Other Churches
3. Homes of Church
   Members
4. Zoos; Places of Historical Interest
5. Institutions

*He's Got the Whole
World in His Hands*
1. Creepers and Crawlers
   (insects)
2. Our Sisters and Brothers
   the Animals (pets)
3. Sun, Moon, and Stars
4. You and Me (friends)

Goal-oriented studies.—Families know about setting goals. In little and big ways, families effect change by setting and achieving goals. The goal-oriented approach to designing extended family events is beneficial in that it provides family members with information and skills for personal growth and for family growth.

What's Important?
1. Values Education
   (laughing at our idols)
2. Money
3. Leisure
4. Health
5. Age

School Days
1. How Children Learn
2. How Youth Learn
3. How Adults Learn
4. How We Learn Together
5. Planning Learning for All
   Ages Together

Family Problems
1. Self Worth
2. Communication
3. Sexuality
4. Problem-Solving
5. Discipline

Family Inventories
1. Likes and Dislikes
2. Unused Strengths
3. Goals for Improving Things
   and Using Family Strengths
4. Family's Involvement in
   Church

Instructional studies.—"Let's learn something new and different!" "Okay! What shall we learn?" It is difficult to imagine a group of people sitting down to plan a unit of study and coming up with a blank sheet of paper. It is difficult

What Happened to Eden?
   (Ecology)
1. Air Pollution
2. Water Pollution
3. Earth Pollution
4. Waste or Stewardship

Celebrate Books
1. Libraries
2. Children's Books
3. Books for All Ages
4. The Book of Books
   (translations of Bible)

What's In a Name?
1. Known by Our Names
   (personal names)
2. The Record-Keeper
   (records of names,
   baptisms, marriages,
   and deaths)
3. Old Testament Names
4. New Testament Names

The Places Where We Live
1. Celebrate the Farm
2. Celebrate the Town
3. Celebrate the City
4. Celebrate the State
5. Celebrate the Country

to imagine that there is "nothing new under the sun" for extended families to learn. The world of information is growing larger book by book, article by article, discovery by discovery. The extended family group can capitalize on this wealth of knowledge. Families can study the Bible, study missionary endeavors, study conservation and ecology, study the community, study the neighborhood, study the world almanac—even the telephone book.

The Duration of the Extended Family

The extended family is a short-term group. It can be offered simultaneously with other short-term studies or at different seasons of the year as the need for an intergenerational group arises. A length of time which seems suitable to churches that operate on a quarterly basis is for the group to exist for thirteen weeks. A short-term intergenerational group could be held during the four-week holiday of Thanksgiving through Christmas—or during the six weeks prior to Easter. Another idea is to use the short-term group in the summer months when attendance is low. Or bring all the age groups together for a "Summer Family" group. One of the positive features of this short-term study model is that the group knows it is existing for a specified number of weeks.

What about retreats? The building of relationships among members needs more time than the weekend or five-day retreat allows, but a retreat is a good event in which to introduce the extended family concept. The retreat or workshop setting is an excellent environment for training.

Frequency and Time-Span of the Gatherings

If the extended family experience is a part of the educational ministry and meets within the time limits of other groups, a session ranges from forty-five minutes to an hour and a half. A workable time centers around an hour. Although activities vary from session to session, the following time allotments will suggest a pattern to follow.

10 minutes—informal chit chat and refreshments
30 minutes—learning activities at each table or in small
              groups following the weekly theme
10 minutes—Bible-related activity
10 minutes—worship/celebration with entire group

Weekly sessions are often supplemented with picnics, potluck suppers, and similar extracurricular activities.

Extended family groups can meet at any time during the week that is convenient. Some groups meet on Sunday evenings during the hour for training, and some meet in the midweek when other activities are scheduled (supper, choir, mission groups, and prayer periods). One of the advantages of meeting in time slots that are already structured is that some people are accustomed to coming to church and their patterns of attendance are set. Another advantage is that the nursery facilities and other groups are available for family members who may not be participating in the extended family experience. From the economic and housekeeping viewpoints, the church facilities are open and heated/cooled/lighted for other groups besides the extended family. In times of energy-money crisis, this is a point of consideration.

The Location

Where shall we put the extended family? They are big (between twenty-five and fifty), they are noisy (giggles and hand-clapping), they use lots of space (big groups, little groups, tables, stages), and they are highly active (move around, eat, and spill juice). Where shall they meet? The extended family needs space. Members need to *see* one another as one big happy family. A large fellowship hall area, a part of an activities building, a large conference room, an outdoor grassy area—these are good spots. Because the small groups are all formed in the same large room, they do not need little cubicles or little classrooms off to the sides. Because the group is large, the home setting has not been as conducive to this model. Most persons do not have playrooms, basements, or attics that will hold the group comfortably. By utilizing the physical facilities of the church, the needs for space, equipment, and janitorial services are easily met.

The extended family members need a place to "hang their hats," but they are a group who *can* and *do* learn in a variety of locations. The group is by no means confined to one place and it is good to look for unusual, unique, and interesting locations to hold some of the sessions. One extended family met at a picnic shelter for Easter sunrise activities. The breakfast of fried apples, bacon, sausage, scrambled eggs, homemade bread, coffee, and juice was prepared by the scoutmaster, his wife, and their teenage children. Everything was cooked over an open fire. The forty members of the extended family celebrated the resurrection "on the first day of the week, at early dawn" in the great out-of-doors.

___ 5. Publicize the Event

The church bulletin and weekly newsletter are two information sheets that reach most of the families in the church. Utilize these sources by placing announcements in them several weeks prior to the mailing of letters or telephoning. Let the basic information become known.

Examples of announcements are given below. In the italicized portions, substitute information which applies to your particular group.

Bulletin Announcement No. 1
Sunday, March 5 we will begin plans for an extended family group. An extended family is a group of persons at all ages meeting together for worship, fellowship,

study, and training. The next *two Sunday evenings* will
be spent in forming the group and planning a calendar
of activities. The group will meet regularly each *Sunday
evening from March through May*. Other activities will
be scheduled at periodic times.

- The group will be made up of all ages—children
  through senior adults.
- Both married and single persons are welcomed.
- The participation of the entire family unit is encouraged.
- An extended family may have a wide variety of 20-
  35 persons. If more are interested another group may
  be formed.

Bulletin Announcement No. 2

"What Is a *Second Family?*"

- Choosing to be a part of a bigger, broader family
  pattern.
- Building bridges between the generations.
- A five-year-old finding a new grandfather, and a sev-
  enty-year-old finding a new grandson.
- A group of people living out the meaning of the
  household of faith.
- All ages finding new ways of talking to each other.
- Every person, no matter what age, a teacher and
  learner.
- Discovering our unique family patterns and sharing
  them with others.
- A person away from home finding a new family.

A *Second Family* group is being formed (date, place,
time). This group will meet from *March through May*.
All are welcomed.

In addition to announcements in printed sources, the
word-of-mouth publicity is of great value. Talking with individuals about the concept not only helps to get the information out but it also allows for feedback, hints, and suggestions
as to how the group can most effectively meet needs.

As the time draws near for the first sessions, posters and

announcements in classes remind persons of the date, place, and time of the meetings.

Reminder: Keep the invitation to join the extended family open to everyone. There is always room for those who respond from this open invitation. The extended family is not a closed or select group even though it is suggested that an intentional effort be made to contact and enlist persons who will form a core which is representative of all ages.

___ 6. Seek Commitments

Before the first session begins, the extended family group should have a nucleus. Much of the success of the group will depend on securing commitments from enough persons to assure a good age distribution and a workable size—numerically speaking. Some individuals and families will respond from the open invitations to join but they cannot be counted in the nucleus. They will be unknown until the first few sessions. To gather some indication of "who" and "how many" will form the extended family group, mail out letters and wait for responses to be returned. If there are some persons who need an additional contact by telephone, call them prior to the first session.

If a list has been compiled of persons who have expressed an interest in this group, there may be more than enough families on this list for the first mailout. Contact these families first. Then make a churchwide distribution if necessary.

The italicized portions of the following letters will need to be changed to fit your specific plans. The times, dates, and program topics are left in these samples to provide additional suggestions as you plan.

Letter No. 1

Dear _____,

By now, we hope you have read in the church bulletin about the *Second Family* that is forming. In order to finalize our plans, we would like to know by *Sunday morning, September 7,* if you would like to participate. The intergenerational group will meet once a week for an hour and a half on a night and at a time the group selects. These decisions will be made at the pre-session planning meeting on *Sunday evening, September 7, 6:00 P.M., Fellowship Hall.* The main headquarters for the *Second Family* will be the church, but there are times when we will meet in other locations for special events.

The coordinating team, composed of *(supply names),* has already met to design a basic framework. The activities and study will center around ideas which can be understood by children as well as adults, and youth. Tentative program ideas range from *the meaning of the family, to touring different churches, to focusing on the life cycles, to celebrating harvesttime and the birthday of Jesus.*

Each person will be asked to serve on a team to conduct one session. We will include light refreshments in most of our get-togethers. Commitment to this experience includes regular attendance, leading one session (working with a team), and active participation in each session.

I believe *Second Family* is one way we can accomplish the goal of building closer bonds of friendship among our church community. I sincerely hope you can be a part of this experience. If you will participate, please return the enclosed card by mail or put it in the offering plate prior to *Sunday morning, September 7.*

Sincerely,

Chairperson, Coordinating Team,
Second Family

Enclosed card for response:

To: *SECOND FAMILY COORDINATING TEAM*
I will participate in *Second Family* by attending, lead-

ing with a team, and involving myself in the activities
of each session.

Name of each family member: Age Group

_____   _____

_____   _____

_____   _____

_____   _____

_____   _____

Age groups: 1-5, 6-11, 12-17, 18-30, 31-40, 41-50, over
           50

____ 7. Finalize the Plans

As the items on the checklist are marked off, the extended
family gets closer to becoming a "real" group. Anticipation
of the first meeting puts pressure on the coordinating team
to put finishing touches on the frameworks.

The process for planning and conducting extended family
experiences are summarized under the following six points.
Provide copies of this process to family members. It will
help them as they plan for weekly sessions with their team.

Process for Planning and Conducting
Extended Family Experiences

1. A large room is needed for flexible room arrangements and grouping. (The fellowship hall in most
   churches would be suitable.)
2. The larger group is divided into smaller groups of
   six to eight persons. Each group should have a table
   to work around. *Do not divide the group into sepa-*
   rate rooms. Each group should have a wide age rep-
   resentation—children, youth, adults.
3. Programming should be flexible with a lot of latitude
   for moving around and spontaneous happenings.
   Leadership should facilitate the learning process of
   the entire group, but let the particular style of process develop at each table. Time allotments will vary
   but may have similar patterns each week.
   10 minutes   Informal chitchat and refreshments.

- 30 minutes   Learning activities at each table following weekly theme. (Learning methods are concrete, action-oriented and experiential.)
- 10 minutes   Bible-related activity.
- 10 minutes   Worship/celebration (with entire group).
4. Study materials may be developed from a combination of preschool, children, and youth materials.
5. Programming should take into account special seasons of the year, holidays, birthdays, and other family occasions.
6. Leadership should be shared as much as possible among all members of the "family." Adults and older youth will need to take primary responsibilities but children should be encouraged to be a part of planning and conducting weekly sessions.

Beginnings! Beginnings are important. Plan thoroughly for the first session. Be aware that the time together will probably be hectic, exciting, loud, and, perhaps, even frustrating and disappointing. There is always so much to do and so much going on. Do not become discouraged at the beginning—especially if this is the first attempt at intergenerational grouping. It is different from working with age-group classes.

Middle! The middle is important. Make it the best. Along the way, take opportunities to get feedback from the extended family members—young and old. Find out what they like, what they do not like, what could be repeated or eliminated. The evaluations can be informal. Perhaps at the end of each session, the question might be: "How did it go tonight?" Wait for responses. Encourage openness and honesty as the members evaluate their experience. Learn from the evaluations. Use what is learned to make the rest of the sessions more satisfying.

Ending! Endings are important. Plan for the ending just as thoroughly as for the first session. The extended family is intended to end. It is a part of the plan. Make the final session or a post-session event a meaningful time together. Provide for love to abound, sadness or relief to be expressed. At the end, evaluate. Evaluations may be informal or formal, but they are very important to learning.

An informal evaluation in which all persons participate.—Provide construction paper, colored pens, scissors, and masking tape. On one wall, prepare a background on which the evaluation papers can be taped. Instruct each family member to choose one or two words which describe their feelings about the entire extended family experience. Have them write these words on the constructed paper. They may wish to decorate or cut designs out of the paper. Ask the family members, one-by-one, in turn, to tape their evaluations to the background which has been prepared. They may wish to share a few sentences or read the words. Remember younger members do not know how to read or write. Allow the activity to become what the members are feeling; lively and gay, solemn and worshipful, sad and teary—let the mood flow with the feeling.

Formal evaluation in which all members can participate.—A formal evaluation tool can be used. One extended family had a post-session potluck supper just for the expressed purpose of evaluating the event. The younger children were not a part of this evaluation, but they were asked, prior to the meeting, to share with their parents the feelings they had about the group. The parents brought those reports to the meeting. Older children, youth, and adults composed the evaluating group. After the potluck supper, each person was given an opportunity to answer questions on a prepared worksheet. Then small groups were formed. One person in each small group recorded on newsprint the statements from the group. The small groups then joined together and the recorders shared their group's statements. The evaluation sheets from each person were collected. Within a week's time the reports were compiled, duplicated, and mailed to the extended family members.

A sample evaluation sheet indicates four major questions to which members responded.

"My Feelings About the Extended Family Experience"
1. What happened to me?
   a. I liked . . .
   b. I didn't like . . .
2. What happened to others? (Share positive and negative insights.)
3. What have I learned? What could I tell someone else who was considering an extended family?
4. Based on what I have learned, what would I do differently next time?

Final evaluation by leadership and/or adult family members.—As the extended family ends, the final evaluations can be used to rebuild other group experiences. The learning from each experience will strengthen the next experience. If possible, put the evaluation and suggestions for doing other extended family groups in some printed form. New leaders, new participants, and interested observers will benefit from this information.

6
Study, Worship, Work, and Play:
Activities and Resources

They have eyes—give them something to see:
    colors, textures, shapes . . .
They have ears—give them something to hear:
    stories, songs, noises . . .
They have noses—give them something to
smell:
    baked bread, paints, flowers . . .
They have hands—give them room to move:
    walk, run, march . . .
They have minds, imaginations, feelings—
    give them time to think,
        time to dream,
            time to cry . . .
They have spirits which need to soar—
    give them ways to use their wings!

Thank You, God

One Friday evening, I was passing through the town where one of my non-kin extended families live and I made an unexpected, unscheduled weekend visit. On Saturday morning, my friends had planned to make a photograph-taking nature hike into the Smoky Mountains. I was invited. Great idea! One problem! I had not come prepared to hike—I only had sandal shoes. One of the daughters, whose shoe size was the same as mine, offered her tennis shoes. She got them. I pulled on a pair of her tube socks and put on the shoes. Same size, nice color, but they sure didn't fit well. Her shoes toed in and my toes went out. Her shoes were worn on the outside of the heel and my shoes usually wear out first toward the inside of the heel. My legs seemed to be leaning in the wrong direction. I gratefully thanked her for offering the shoes, but I declined wearing them. I hiked, very slowly and carefully, in my own flimsy sandals.

The following program suggestions for an extended family group are offered to you with the same spirit of sharing that prompted my teenage friend to volunteer her tennis shoes. The ideas are given with the knowledge they may not fit your purposes. Some of the activities you can adapt. Some of the ideas will stimulate your thinking. It would be great if all of the suggestions would work for you.

The program suggestions are written in detail. There are approximate time limits, purposes for each activity, explanations as to how activities meet certain objectives, and even questions and statements that can be used verbatim in leading the activities and discussions. A model of learning and teaching is being presented in written form.

The sessions are arranged to form a unit of study or a theme—"Thank you, God." The first session focuses on getting acquainted and planning ahead. The second session builds on the family systems mentioned in chapter 2.

Sessions three and four are designed to show the activity-oriented teaching and learning process. The topics of food and birthdays are just two subjects which are of common interest to people of all ages. Sessions that you design can be added to these first four.

The final session includes activities for evaluation and closure. It can be used as a fifth session or as the final session of any extended family event.

SESSION 1
Thank You, God, . . . for Many Names
Session goal: To acquaint members with one another, form leadership teams, and plan future sessions

Before the Session

• Arrange the room with tables and chairs distributed in a U-shape.

• Make necessary arrangements for refreshments.

• Secure supplies: newsprint, poster board, chalkboard, colored marker pens, construction paper for name tags, masking tape, scissors.

• (Optional—Duplicate and provide copies of Sessions 2, 3, 4, and 5. Have these copies available to give the leadership teams to aid their planning.)

• (Optional—Secure record player and record: "What Is Your Name?" by Hap Palmer, side 2, *Learning Basic Skills Through Music*, Vol. 1, 1969. Activity Records, Educational Activities, Inc., Freeport, L.I., New York 11520. Or, use other songs which center around names and learning of names.)

• Review the Scripture passage and worship suggestions.

During the Session

1. *Refreshments* (Large group) As family members arrive, direct them to the refreshment table. Since the emphasis is on names, place placards in front of the food. Print the names of food in bold letters so younger children can read the words. Tell the names of foods to nonreaders.

2. *"Where Is My Family?"* (Small groups) Purpose: To practice forming small family units. (5 minutes)

Get the attention of the members as they mingle at the refreshment table—blow a whistle, yell, or flip off the lights. It is time to begin!

Instruct them to gather around the tables, forming a family-like group of eight persons. Several children, a youth, a mother, a father, a grandparent, an aunt or an uncle—all ages and generations should be represented in each small group. Ask members of immediate families to separate. (Small children usually prefer to stay with someone they know—parent or sibling.) The facilitators will need to assist this formation by moving persons to other tables as needed in order to achieve a good balance.

After the family units are seated, ask them to look around the room. Discuss the formation process. Tell them these family units will vary from week to week, but the process will be the same each time instructions are given to "make yourselves into a family unit or small group." If other group arrangements are desired, specific instructions will be given at that time.

3. *"My Name Is . . ."* (Small groups) Purpose: To learn the first names and nicknames. (15 minutes)

(Prior to the session, place the following materials in the center of each table: colored marker pens, construction paper, scissors, and masking tape.)

(a) Instruct the family members to make name tags for themselves. Tell them to use first names only and to use the name that they wish to be called in this extended family group. (This name may or may not be their usual name.) Tell them to print their name and, if they wish and if there is time, they may decorate their name tag by drawing something which tells about their hobbies, interests, talents, and so forth. Tape the name tag where all can see it.

(b) When the name tags are completed, ask each person (one at a time, going all around the table) to share his or her name. Almost everyone has had a nickname or has wanted a certain nickname. Ask each person to talk about their nickname. If a member does not have a nickname, the group can help them choose one. Encourage them to choose a nickname which tells something about their positive features—a horseshoe champ could be Ringer or Champ, a musician called Melody, so on. Remind the family members to listen carefully and learn the nicknames. Later they will make introductions using the first name and nickname.

4. *"I Would Like to Introduce . . ."* (Large group) Purpose: To introduce each person to the extended family, using first names and nicknames—get-acquainted activity. (15 minutes)

After the name tags and small group introductions are completed, instruct the members to turn in their chairs so they can see the facilitator and everyone else in the extended family. Beginning with one table and going around the group, let each person introduce the person seated to the right. Introductions are to be made by giving the person's first name (name they wish to be called), plus information concerning their nickname.

(Optional: Play record "What Is Your Name?" by Hap Palmer. Within the text of the song, the leader points to different persons during the pause in the singing. Individuals are to yell out their name when the leader points to them. Sing other songs that focus on names, if time allows.)

5. *"The Name of the Game Is—Touch Blue."* (Large group) Purpose: To get the members up and moving around. (Use if time permits and if members need a break.) (5-10 minutes)

People have names. Objects have names. Ask members to stand. They will move around for this activity. Tell them to listen to the name of an object as the leader says: "Touch *(object)."* They are to find the object, touch it, freeze in place, and stop talking. When everyone is touching an object, the group will look like frozen statues—silent and in weird positions.

The leader will call out another object and the members move to find it. Repeat the process. The following list gives examples: Touch something blue, touch a man's wristwatch, touch a woman's brown shoe, touch a pair of eyeglasses (carefully), touch a wedding ring—add your own!

6. *"Add My Name—I'll Help!"* (Large group—small groups) Purpose: To plan future sessions and form teams who will take charge of the weekly planning and programming duties. (15-30 minutes)

On a large poster board, chalkboard, or newsprint, write the theme and session titles for the upcoming family meetings. (If specific program ideas, such as the five sessions given in this book, are not being used, brainstorm with the members about topics they wish to consider. Choose enough topics to fit the number of weeks for which planning must be done.) Do not put dates by the topics yet. Do create an interest in the topics. If copies of program ideas have been prepared, distribute these among the members. Let them flip through the ideas. Something may spark an interest.

After the topics are listed, ask members to choose the ones that interest them. Explain that those who are interested in the same topic will become a leadership team to plan and carry out the program for one session. Ask for volunteers, topic by topic. Write down the names. (Keep a mixture of ages on each team. If one topic fills up with five or six persons on the team, move some persons toward their second choice.)

After the leadership teams have been formed, ask these persons to form small "huddle" groups. Let them decide on some dates when they could be in charge.

Call the "huddle" groups to attention and ask them to now help set up the calendar. Who will lead on what dates? Beside the topics, write down the dates as they are called out from the groups. Some juggling of topics and dates and teams will be necessary in order to get everyone working together on a schedule. This process of juggling is done by consensus and cooperation. It takes time but sets a model for working together that is important in family life.

This model or process of planning the programs can be used at every new beginning of an extended family experience. This process is what is meant by "filling in the framework." It involves sharing leadership duties among all ages. It involves placing one's name on the line—a commitment to help.

7. *"Called by My Name . . ."* (Large group) Purpose: To worship and study the Bible. (10 minutes)

In a modern translation or paraphrase, read 2 Chronicles 7:11-22. Focus on verse 14—"If my people who are called by my name." Give the context for the phrase. God was promising Solomon that he (God) would dwell in the newly-built Temple as long as the people humbled themselves, sought him, and prayed to him. In simple terms and in concrete thought patterns (so the children will understand), talk about the blessings and promises that are available to this extended family group—people who believe in God and who are called by his name. Encourage the members to come together, as the children of God, to relate, love, learn, and live in his family of faith.

SESSION 2
Thank You, God, . . . for Our Family

Session goal: To focus on the family systems in which each person has a role and to help group members develop a feeling that "we are becoming a family." (See chapter 2)

Before the Session

• Make necessary room arrangements. Arrange tables and chairs for small family units. Set up one area for the display of baby pictures.

• Assign a person the responsibility of receiving the baby pictures, making a record of whose picture goes with which number, arranging the pictures in numbered sequence on a table.

• Secure maps of the United States. (One will be needed for each small group.) Mount on cardboard.

• Secure supplies: straight pins, ½ x 1 inch pieces of colored paper, fine-point felt-tip pens, pencils, white paper, newsprint or large poster board, Polaroid cameras and film.

• Assignment prior to session: By post card or telephone call, remind members to bring a baby picture.

• Assign several persons the task of taking Polaroid shots.

During the Session

1. *Refreshments* (Large group) Provide refreshments that represent the food families—vegetables (carrot/celery sticks), fruit (apple slices/orange sections), meat and fish (finger sandwiches of luncheon meat and tuna salad), grain (bread in sandwiches and crackers), milk and produce (cheese cubes and milk to drink). Label foods according to their family grouping.

2. *"The Family Album"* (Large group) Purpose: To get better acquainted with members and to focus upon the family of origin. (10-15 minutes)

As family members arrive, ask them to give their baby pictures to the person who will place a numbered slip of paper on the picture and record the number and name of person. (As the Family Album display is being set up, family members may visit the refreshment table, or begin work on the second activity, The Family Map, and then come back to the Family Album activity.)

(a) Family members will be given paper and pencil. Instruct them to mingle at the baby picture display, identify the pictures, record the number and name of person. (Adults and youth will assist younger children.)

(b) If necessary, call time. Bring the members back to the work tables. Read the names of pictures from the master list and hold up the pictures at the same time. Recognize the persons with the most correct responses.

(c) Call attention to the family of origin and the importance of this family group to our development.

3. *"The Family Map"* (Small groups) Purpose: To locate the relatives and "kin folks" of group members and focus upon the function of an extended family. (20 minutes)

(Prior to the activity, place the following materials at each table: large map of U.S., pieces of colored paper (one color per person, 10-12 rectangles of each color), felt-tip pens, and straight pins.)

(a) Form into family units around the work tables. Tell each person to choose a stack of colored paper and write his or her name on them. These are identification markers. Instruct them to locate the city or town where they have relatives who are extended family—grandparents, parents, aunts, sisters, etc. Place an identification marker on the spot, secure with a straight pin.

(b) When the family units have completed their tasks, ask them to look at their maps, discuss locations, distance from relatives, amount of time spent with these persons, and favorite activities when they are together. The leader may wish to direct the discussion and focus on the importance of the extended family.

4. *"The Family Tree"* (Small groups-Large group) Purpose: To build group spirit among the new family members by joining in a group project. (20 minutes)

(Prior to the activity have the following materials available at the work tables: newsprint or poster board for background, marker pens, cameras and film, white paper, pencils, Bibles, and songbooks)

Divide the group into four work teams:

1. Design family tree background, add pictures as the roving photographers make Polaroid shots of immediate families or individuals.

2. Select and/or compose family song and cheer.

3. Choosing Scripture verse to represent family.

4. Compose a motto for the extended family.

5. (Optional: Select a name for the extended family, if this was not done earlier.)

Allow time for the small groups to work, then draw them back into the large group to share their efforts. If possible, make a display somewhere in the room or a hallway of the church, combining the family tree, name, motto, song, cheer, and Scripture reference. Perhaps a team will need to work on this after the session.

5. *"The Family Portrait"* (Large group) Purpose: To allow members to "behold" the extended family group as it is portrayed in *real* living color. (10 minutes)

(a) Use the activity found on p. 60, chapter 3, or

(b) Instruct the family members to form a large circle and join hands. Ask the members to "behold" the circle—look around, acknowledge others with the eyes, get acquainted by visually perceiving one another. Tell the group that this is the family portrait in living, moving color.

(c) After either suggestion (a) or (b), debrief the activity by sharing the assumption that the extended family is for all ages, interacting together as family members (see chapter 3). Ask the family members to move together into a tightly-knit circle, arms entwined. Sing together, pray together. Celebrate the extended family in a manner which has meaning to the members.

SESSION 3
Thank You, God, . . . for Birthdays

Session goal: To celebrate a common experience of life—being born.

Before the Session

Since half of the fun in a birthday party is the planning and expectation, allow family members to share in the party preparation. Bring all the supplies to the session and divide into work teams. After the preparation is finished—then comes "celebration time."

• Secure decorations for the room and tables: balloons, streamers, centerpieces, supplies for party hats.

• Secure refreshments befitting a party—cakes, cupcakes, ice creams, soft drinks, candy.

• Secure supplies for activities: empty boxes (wrapped in birthday paper/bows), tokens, strips of paper.

• Preview Scriptures and closing worship suggestions.

During the Session

1. *Refreshments* (Large group) Prepare food ahead of time, but leave last-minute preparations for members to do: arrange centerpieces, cut cake, fill cups, etc. The refreshments will be a major part of the celebration. Plan for candles to be blown out!

2. *Decorations* (Large group) Everyone can be involved in decorating—blowing up balloons, taping up streamers, making table decorations. If supplies are furnished, let each one make a party hat. Offer a prize for the best hat, funniest hat, etc.

3. *Music* (Large group) Singing goes with parties. Select happy songs, action songs, include traditional birthday songs and poems. Ask members to share any poems or songs that are a part of their own birthday tradition.

4. *Activities/Games* (Large group) Two activities are suggested, but any games can be used. These activities are best used with groups of 12-15 persons. (Because each person takes a turn, the time factor must be considered.)

"My Imaginary Birthday Gift"

Purpose: To learn more about one another by asking family members to reveal what would make them happy.

Supplies needed: large, empty box wrapped in birthday paper

Process: Family members sit in a circle. Each person has a turn by rotating to the right; or as a person finishes a turn, he or she may place the box in the hands of a person whom they choose to be next. Give the following instructions: "This box contains an imaginary gift of your choosing. The gift can be anything in the world—any size, shape, color. The gift will make you very, very happy . . . right now. Tell us what is in the box and why this gift will make you happy."

"Gifts I've Never Received"

Purpose: Players reveal what gifts they *have not received* and learn about gifts that other family members *have received.* The purpose of the game is to make other players give up their tokens first. The player with the most tokens left (or the last to run out) is the winner.
Supplies needed: large, empty box wrapped in birthday paper with a slot cut in top; tokens—pennies, macaroni, toothpicks, small pieces of paper. (Each person needs as many tokens as there are persons playing. If fifteen people play, each player needs fifteen tokens.)
Process: Family members sit in a circle. Box is placed in the center to receive tokens. Each player is given as many tokens as there are players in the group. Give the following instructions: Each player, in turn, is to think of a gift they have never received for a birthday present. The secret is to think of a gift that you hope everyone else has received but which has not been one of your own gifts. The first player to begin says: "I have never received a _____ for my birthday." All players who have received that gift, get up and put one of their tokens in the box. If players have never received the gift, they hold on to their tokens. The second player repeats: "I have never received a _____ for my birthday." And so the play continues until time runs out or one player is left with tokens.

5. *Closing Worship* (Large group) Purpose: To give family members an opportunity to affirm one another by giving imaginary gifts and to focus on the gift that God gives each one.

As the family members join together for the closing worship, give each person several small slips of paper and a pencil. Ask each member to choose several persons to whom they would like to give an imaginary gift. The gift can be anything. Write the gift on the paper (sign a name only if you desire). Give the family members time to distribute their "gifts" and ask the recipients to not open their gift until later.

Share thoughts about the gifts that are mentioned in the following Scriptures: John 4:10, Romans 6:23, 2 Corinthians 9:15. (Remember to bring the abstract concepts down to the level of the children by speaking in concrete terms.) Close with prayer, thanking God for his Son—his Gift too wonderful for words.

SESSION 4
Thank You, God, . . . for Daily Food

Session goal: To lead extended family members to a deeper appreciation for daily food.

Before the Session

• Prepare an interest center with jars of home-canned fruit and vegetables, green vegetable plants (herbs in pots, patio tomato plants), boxes of crackers, flour, sugar, etc.

• Arrange the tables and chairs for small groups. Cover the tables with paper or disposable cloths.

• Secure and prepare food for the taste-smell activity. Have one person at each table prepared to assist with the activity. Provide blindfolds. Suggested pieces of food: carrot slices, green or black olives, cucumber slices, apple slices, berries of any kind, cherries, watermelon chunks, citrus fruit sections, banana slices, pineapple chunks, potato slices, and other items available to you. Prepare enough pieces for at least two taste-tests per person.

• Prepare dips for the foods and batter for unleavened bread.

• Secure supplies: containers for collection of fresh fruits and vegetables, paring knives for each table, electric skillets, large platters, bowls for scapes, forks, dessert plates, napkins.

• Preview the Scriptures and enlist readers for the worship.

• Prior to the session: By announcement, by post card or

telephone, ask each person to bring an item of fresh food—fruit or vegetable.

During the Session

1. *"Filling the Baskets"* As family members enter, ask them to place their items of fruit or vegetable in the basket. Just before the session begins, distribute the food equally among the work tables.

2. *"Hum-a-Tune"* (Small groups) Purpose: To give small groups a task which draws attention to the topic. (10 minutes)

Ask family members to form small family units at the work tables. Ask each family unit to select a tune which mentions a food, rehearse the song, and be ready to sing it for the others. Give the groups time to complete their assignments. Call them together for the sharing time. (Suggested tunes: "Can She Bake a Cherry Pie, Billie Boy?" "Tea for Two," "Found a Peanut," "On the Good Ship Lollypop," "Yes, We Have No Bananas," "Don't Sit Under the Apple Tree.")

3. *"Taste-Smell Test"* (Small groups) Purpose: To help members appreciate the role that the senses play in the enjoyment of food. (15 minutes)

(Prior to this activity, provide each table with a blindfold and a *covered* platter of sample foods.)

One at a time, each member will be blindfolded and handed a piece of food. They may smell the food and make a guess. They may eat the food and make a guess. Give the following instructions to the taster: "Take this piece of food. Gently feel the food. Raise it to your nose, sniff the food, try to remember the smell. What is the food? (If the guess is incorrect, continue.) Place the food in your mouth, taste it, try to recognize the taste. Take your time. Enjoy the taste. What is the food?"

Do as many tests as time will allow. Save left-over food for the feast. Debrief the experience by asking questions: What was the best part of the experience? When did you first remember the food? Or, was it a new food? Do you like or dislike the food you received? Would you rather have had a food given to someone else? What would happen in this test if the sense of smell was not used? What part does sight play in the enjoyment of food?

4. *"The Family Feast"* (Small groups) Purpose: To celebrate by preparing the food, reading and hearing Scriptures that pertain to food, and eating the food. (30 minutes)

(Prior to this activity, provide electric skillets—one for every two tables, the batter and oil for frying, the containers of fruits and vegetables, several knives, serving platters, scrape bowls, eating utensils, napkins, dips.)

Instruct each group to pare, slice, and arrange the food on platters. Select someone to prepare the unleavened bread. Encourage all members to participate. Ask that no one eat until the feast begins. As the food is being prepared, suggest the members talk about the food, the scrapes, the leftovers, the need for food, the lack of food.

When the food is prepared and one piece of unleavened bread has been fried for each member, invite the family to the feast. Tell them the celebration continues with the symbolic eating and worship. Remind them that certain foods have been and are important in the religious ceremonies of people from all over the world. Instruct the members to listen to the reading of the Scriptures and then to take one small taste of the food that has been mentioned. After the worship, the food may be consumed in greater quantities.

"Come to the Feast, My Family"

Blessing
   Read: Psalm 104:27-28 *
The Unleavened Bread
   Read: Exodus 12:31,34
            (Each person breaks off and eats a piece of bread.)

* For all Scriptures, Revised Standard Version is preferable.

The Vegetables and Fruits
  Read: Deuteronomy 11:10-12
      (Each person eats a piece of vegetable.)
  Read: Psalm 1:1-3
      (Each person eats a piece of fruit.)
The Herbs, Milk, and Honey
  Read: Proverbs 15:17
      (Each person tastes the herb dip.)
  Read: Exodus 3:7-8
      (Each person tastes the honey-cream dip.)

After the worship, continue the celebration by passing the food and eating until it is all gone. (Encourage all family members to assist in the clean-up tasks.)

Recipes

Unleavened Bread: Combine the dry ingredients: ⅓ cup of 100% whole wheat flour, ½ teaspoon baking powder, 1 teaspoon sugar, ⅛ teaspoon salt. Add: 1 teaspoon oil and ⅓ cup water. Mix until smooth. To make patties, pour one tablespoon of the batter onto a hot, greased electric fry pan or griddle. Cook until bubbles appear on the top, and the bottom is lightly browned. Flip and finish cooking. Frying time: approximately 6 minutes. Servings: 9 two-inch patties per recipe.

Honey-Cream Dip for Fruit: Combine: ½ cup mayonnaise, 2 tablespoon liquid honey. Fold in to the above: 1 cup heavy cream, whipped. Makes 2½ cups.

Herb Dip for Vegetables: Mix together: 1 cup mayonnaise, 1 raw beaten egg yolk, dashes of A-1 sauce, Worchestershire sauce, French mustard, hot sauce, lemon juice, 4-5 dashes curry powder, salt, pepper. Add: ½ cup sour cream, ⅓ cup snipped parsley (fresh or dried), 2 teaspoons finely chopped green onions, 1 tablespoon anchovy paste (optional), 1 mashed clove garlic, 4-5 drops green food coloring. Mix all ingredients well and chill. Makes 1½ cups.

SESSION 5
Thank You, God, . . . for Memories

Session goal: To look at the past and present of the extended family members and to evaluate the experience in the group by utilizing memories.

Before the Session

• Secure artifacts or photographs that will stimulate memories of the "good old days" and arrange these items into an interest center.

• Arrange a focal point for the Closing Worship.

• Make copies of the worksheet, "My Feelings About the Extended Family Experience." (See chapter 5, p. 118.)

• Secure supplies: ball (basketball, kickball, volleyball) clay or play dough, tin foil, pipe cleaners, white or colored paper, glue, scissors, old magazines, crayons or colored pencils, pencils.

• Make necessary arrangements for presentation of song, "Amazing Grace."

During the Session

1. *Refreshments* (Large group) "I remember how good my mother could cook . . . ." Foods of the old days are good when combined with foods of the modern day. Make up some combinations like old-fashioned gingerbread served with non-dairy topping, milk mixed with instant flavoring, homemade bread with artificial butter, store-bought angel food cake topped with fresh strawberries and "real" whipped cream. Use some talk time to share special memories of good foods and old recipes.

2. *"Memories Are Made of This"* (Small groups) Purpose: To look at the past and to realize that most memories are based around something—an object, a feeling, an event. (20 minutes)

(Prior to this activity, place at each work table some materials which will help members to make pictures, objects, or collages: clay or play dough, tin foil, pipe cleaners, white paper and colored paper, crayons or colored pencils, glue, scissors, old magazines.)

Ask the members to form into small family units at the work tables. Instruct them to select a memory of something out of their past—good or bad—and to pick out the main objects or feelings or events in this memory. (Example: I remember my grandmother having hot homemade bread ready for us when we arrived at her house. The two main objects are hot bread and grandmother. The feeling was delight, happiness.) After each one thinks of a memory, do more than just talk about it—make a picture or collage or an art object. (Example: From clay, mold a loaf of bread, or draw a happy face eating bread, or make a collage from a picture of bread, a grandmother, and a happy face of a child.)

As a large group, share some of the pictures and art objects and memories. Spend a few minutes discussing the value of having a memory. Ask: How far back can you remember? Who will have the most to remember—older or younger persons? Do memories tell us much about ourselves? Can we use memories to plan the future?

3. *"From the Past . . . to the Present"* (Large group) Purpose: To help family members become aware of changes that occur in life by recalling *what used to be* in relation to *what is*—past and present. (20-30 minutes)

Present the song "Amazing Grace" (solo, group singing, tape/record or reading of lyrics). Call special attention to the lines in which the writer John Newton implies: "I once was lost, but now am found; I once was blind, but now I see." Like this songwriter, most people have memories of what we once were in the past and we have some knowledge of what we are now—in the present. Changes occur in life. This next activity will help create an awareness of change.

Ask the family members to stand in a circle. The leader

will give instructions and then toss out the ball to start the activity: The person who is holding the ball will say the following sentence, filling in the blanks from his or her own memory—"I once was _____ but now I am _____." The person with the ball will then bounce the ball to someone else in the circle. This person, who now holds the ball, fills in the statement—"I once was _____ but now I am _____." Repeat the process until everyone has had a turn.

(Examples: I once was three feet tall, but now I am five feet two inches. I once was blond haired, but now I am a brunette. I once was a country person, but now I am a city person.)

Debrief the activity by asking family members to share their thoughts based on questions like: What did you just do? What happened? What have you learned about yourself and others? In ten years, will your statements be different? Will some statements be the same? Share the thoughts expressed in 2 Corinthians 5:17-19. In concrete, simple terms talk about "old things passing away and all things becoming new" when Christ comes into our lives.

4. *"My Memories of Our Extended Family . . ."* (Small groups-large group) Purpose: To lead members in an evaluation of their experiences in the extended family group by asking them to recall special memories. (20 minutes)

Ask the family members to evaluate the extended family experience by recalling some of the events and happenings of the past weeks. Distribute the evaluation worksheets and pencils. Allow time for members to work individually (young children will need assistance in forming evaluations and recording their answers).

Draw the members into small groups and ask each person to share a memory from the worksheet.

Ask the members to join in a circle, bringing their individual worksheets. Gather around the Family Tree or another meaningful symbol of the extended family experience (one extended family group used a large wooden cross). Lead the family members to a closure by inviting them to place their memories (worksheets) on or near the display or focal point. (This may be done one-by-one or as a group.) As the members return to the circle, remind them that leaving the extended family will be experienced differently by the members. In the days to come when the family is separated, the memories will bring the family together again. The apostle Paul often wrote to his Christian friends, "I thank God for every remembrance of you."

Close the time together with prayer, songs, hugs, and handshakes.

Additional Resources

Extra Activities

Alternate or extra activities for extended family sessions are found in chapters 2, 3, and 4.

"My Extended Family"—p. 29

"The Pied Piper"—p. 57

"The Family Portrait"—p. 60

Learning from Experience Activities

Experience Questions—p. 92

Unfinished Sentences—p. 93

Cartoons—p. 94

Lists—p. 94

Program Planning

The following books and resource materials will provide suggestions for planning your extended family experience in the church.

Bock, Lois; and Working, Miji, *Happiness Is a Family Time Together.* Westwood, N.J.: Fleming H. Revell Co., 1975.

Canfield, Jack; and Wells, Harold C., *100 Ways to Enhance*

Self-Concept in the Classroom. Englewood Cliffs, N.J.: Prentice-Hall, Inc., 1976.

Chandler, Russ; and Chandler, Sandie, *Your Family: Frenzy or Fun.* Los Angeles: Action House Publishers, 1977.

Henry, Mark; and Henry, Mary Frances, *A Patchwork Family.* Nashville: Broadman Press, 1978.

Huck, Gabe; and Sloyan, Virginia, eds., *Parishes & Families.* Washington, D.C.: The Liturgical Conference, Inc., 1973.

Jeep, Elizabeth McMahon; and Huck, Gabe, *Celebrate Summer.* New York: Paulist Press, 1973.

Planning Intergenerational Experiences, LS15-323. Order from Judson Book Store, Valley Forge, PA, 19481.

Rogers, Jack; and Rogers, Sharee, *The Family Together: Inter-Generational Education in the Church School.* Los Angeles: Action House Publishers, 1976.

The New Games Book. New Games Foundation, Garden City, N.Y.: Dolphin Books/Doubleday & Company, Inc., 1976.

Your Family: Learning, Loving, Living. An Equipping Center study module (intergenerational and individual family study guides and worksheets). Order from Materials Services Department, 127 Ninth Ave., N., Nashville, TN 37234. $14.95

General Helps

For further study in the area of teaching and learning with all ages together in the church, the following books are suggested.

Bontrager, John, *Free the Child in You.* Philadelphia: Pilgrim Press, 1974.

Duckert, Mary, *Open Education Goes to Church.* Philadelphia: The Westminster Press, 1976.

Freed, Alvyn M. *TA for Kids (and Grownups Too).* Sacramento: Jalmar Press, 1971.

_____, *TA for Teens (and Other Important People)*. Sacramento: Jalmar Press, 1976.

_____, *TA for Tots (and Other Prinzes)*. Sacramento: Jalmar Press, 1973.

Griggs, Don; and Griggs, Pat, *Generations Learning Together*. Livermore, CA: Griggs Educational Service, 1976.

Hendrix, John; and Hendrix, Lela, *Experiential Education: X-Ed*. Nashville: Abingdon Press, 1975.

Huber, Evelyn M., *Doing Christian Education in New Ways*. Valley Forge: Judson Press, 1978.

James, Muriel, *Born to Love: Transactional Analysis in the Church*. Reading, MA: Addison-Wesley Publishing Company, 1973.

_____, *What Do You Do with Them Now That You've Got Them? Transactional Analysis for Moms and Dads*. Reading, MA: Addison-Wesley Publishing Company, 1974.

Koehler, George, *Learning Together: A Guide for Intergenerational Education in the Church*. Nashville: United Methodist Publishing House, 1976.

Satir, Virginia, *Peoplemaking*. Palo Alto: Science and Behavior Books, Inc., 1972.